The Brooklyn Heights PROMENADE

Henrik Krogius

THE History PRESS

Published by The History Press
Charleston, SC 29403
www.historypress.net

All photographs by author unless otherwise noted.

First published 2011

Manufactured in the United States

ISBN 978.1.60949.529.9

Library of Congress CIP data applied for.

Notice: The information in this book is true and complete to the best of our knowledge. It is offered without guarantee on the part of the author or The History Press. The author and The History Press disclaim all liability in connection with the use of this book.

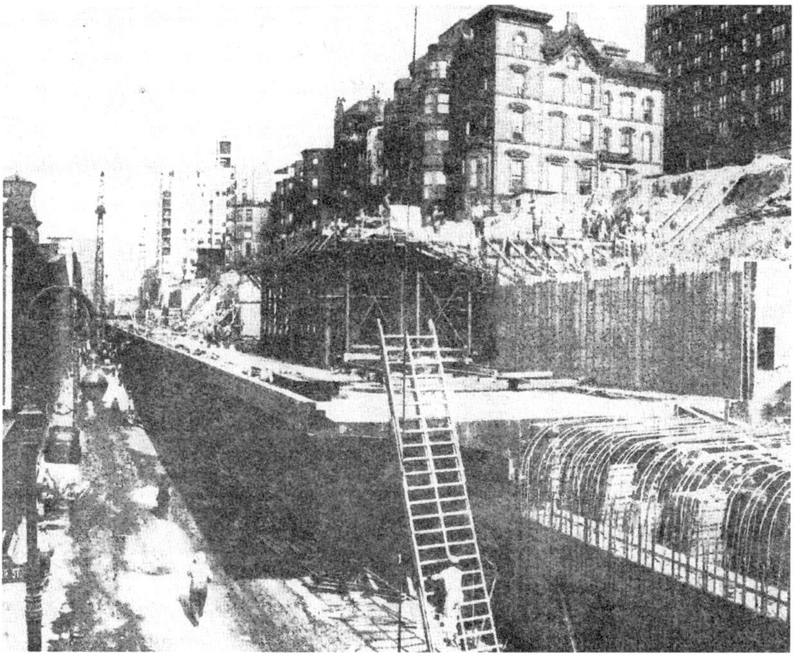

A shelf of the Brooklyn-Queens Expressway cantilever projects dramatically above Furman Street next to the Brooklyn Heights waterfront during construction, probably in late 1947. The house at the top, 222 Columbia Heights, was subsequently demolished and replaced by a new one considerably later. The original print of this photo, lent to the *Brooklyn Heights Press* by the Triborough Bridge and Tunnel Authority and returned, could not be located by that agency upon a subsequent request. Hence, the version shown here is taken from a prior newspaper publication.

Contents

Preface

While a member of a broadcast union on strike against the National Broadcasting Company (NBC) in April 1976, I wrote an article for the weekly *Brooklyn Heights Press* recalling the time when the Heights Promenade was under construction, as well as my attendance at a then rare public meeting at Borough Hall to protest a threat to the Promenade's views that arose only a couple of years after its completion. Publisher J. Dozier Hasty asked me to spend the remaining duration of the strike as acting editor of the *Press*, and he suggested that I write a piece about the Promenade's origins. Easy, I thought. I would simply go to the Long Island Historical Society (now Brooklyn Historical Society) and summarize what I expected to find in the archives.

How chagrined I was to discover the poverty of information on the subject there and elsewhere. What resulted was my sporadic investigation lasting well over a decade in spare hours after I was back at NBC and afterward. Engineers tend to live long lives, and several who had some connection to the Brooklyn-Queens Expressway (BQE) project shared recollections and opinions, as did a former planning commission member and a number of older Heights residents. The three residents most closely involved had died, but some of their letters and preserved documents remained.

A Columbia University graduate planning student named Marina Yu unearthed the transcript of a public hearing that shed some crucial light. As interviews and correspondence elicited claims and counterclaims, I wrote a number of short articles for the *Press* along with a few longer overviews as I arrived closer to a consensus.

The Promenade was so remarkable in pairing a highway to a pedestrian amenity and creating a positive community feature that I thought it might provide an example for other cities bedeviled by the automobile. That idea won me three grants to study urban highway projects in this country and abroad for their possible integration with pedestrian goals. Sadly, however, I found that the particular situation and topography that had allowed for the Promenade was too special a combination for any real replication elsewhere. In Richmond, Virginia; Phoenix, Arizona; and Seattle, Washington, I found patches of park built over highways, and in Paris and a pair of Japanese cities I found highways built across building roofs that permitted a measure of comfort to pedestrians on the streets below, but still I did not find the Promenade's real marriage of motorists' and pedestrians' interests. The closest parallel was up the East River from the Promenade, on the Manhattan side, where Carl Schurz Park and John H. Finley Walk covered part of the Franklin D. Roosevelt Drive—just not quite as elegantly nor with such spectacular effect.

The Heights Promenade remains, then, a feature beyond duplication. That it should have come about as a lucky afterthought, and not by pre-design, is the curious story of these pages.

Part I

The Story of the Promenade

In the Shadow of War

Nobody envisioned such a solution. That is a startling thing about the Brooklyn Heights Promenade—a walkway joined to a highway to provide a public platform for observing one of the world's greatest harbor panoramas.

Also surprising is that the design for this urban marvel was arrived at in deep obscurity, its plans evolving in the midst of World War II when almost all attention was focused elsewhere, and long before the current requirement of New York and many other cities that important projects go through prescribed stages of public scrutiny.

The Promenade emerged as an unintended consequence of the ambition of New York State's most powerful official, the "master builder" Robert Moses, to construct an expressway (a divided highway for commercial and military as well as private vehicles) connecting the boroughs of Brooklyn and Queens. Moses won federal funding for the project on the claim that it was needed for national defense. The Promenade was not part of his original intent, which was to run the highway through the heart of the historic Brooklyn Heights neighborhood.

To be sure, there had been some earlier ideas for turning the outer edge of Brooklyn Heights into space for public enjoyment. In about 1827, the landowner and early developer Hezekiah Pierrepont had

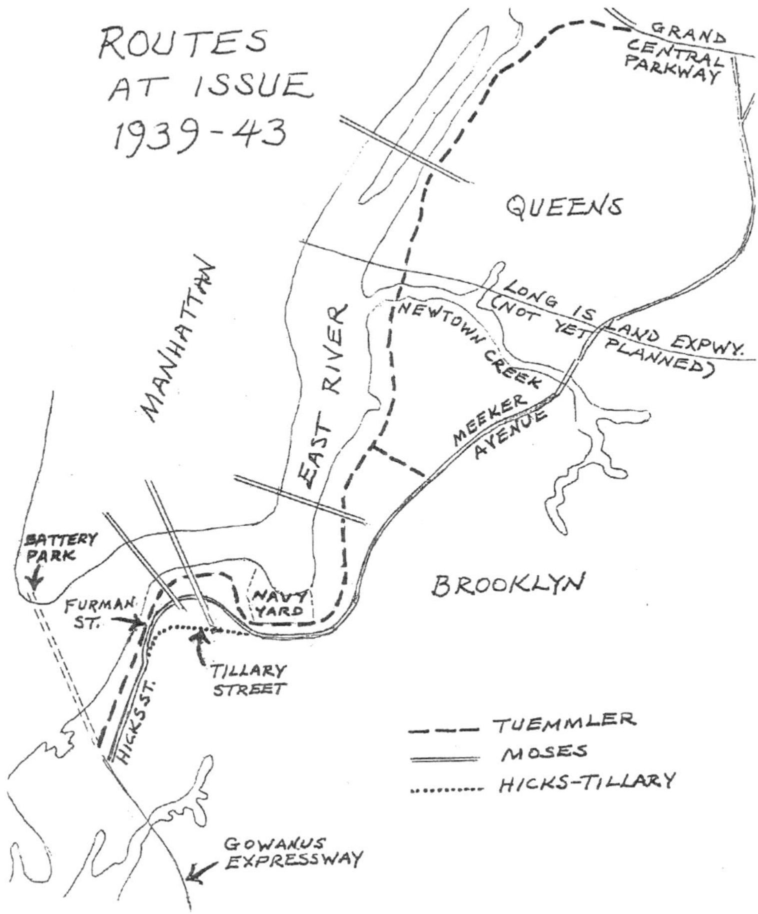

The highway route proposed by City Planning Department engineer Fred Tuemmler generally hewed to the East River shoreline, while the Robert Moses route ran farther inland. The bend into Tillary Street would have bisected the Brooklyn Heights neighborhood. Along Furman Street, the highway ultimately followed a short portion of the route that had also been advocated by Tuemmler.

proposed a promenade atop the Heights embankment facing the East River, but his neighbors along the street known as Columbia Heights, which ran closest to the embankment, refused to cooperate. Some seventy-five years later, there were suggestions to string together the gardens on the roofs of six warehouses on the west, or waterfront, side of Furman Street, at the base of the embankment.

However, by the time World War II broke out, these ideas were far from planners' minds. In 1939, as it happened—before Moses got in on the Brooklyn-Queens highway project—a topographical engineer with the then new City Planning Department, Fred Tuemmler, mapped a Brooklyn-Queens route that hewed close to the shoreline and included Furman Street. Tuemmler even imagined a section with a cantilevered northbound roadway above the southbound Furman lanes—but not with anything like a promenade on top.

Soon after, Moses—who was to claim that he'd never heard of Tuemmler's idea—envisioned a route farther inland that would run in a cut along Hicks Street through what is now called Cobble Hill (and it does run thus—the hated "ditch") and would continue through part of Brooklyn Heights, swinging eastward near Pierrepont Street to connect with Tillary Street. From Tillary it would pursue much the route it does today.

In those days before community planning boards, environmental statements and multiple required hearings, Moses met no effective opposition from south of Atlantic Avenue, a major artery that cuts roughly west–east across the northern third of Brooklyn, but Brooklyn Heights was another matter. The Brooklyn Heights Association was already thirty-two years old, with politically connected lawyers and other savvy professionals on its board, when the *Brooklyn Eagle* blared on September 19, 1942: "Plan for Express Highway Is Shocking." The *Eagle* story noted that "the general route under consideration would cut across Monroe Place and Pierrepont Street in a way that would probably involve the demolition of at least part of the brand-new Appellate Division Courthouse."

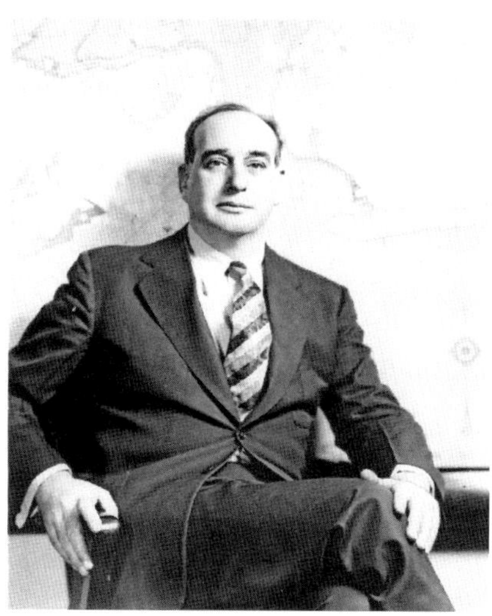

Robert Moses, about the time he was planning the BQE. *Associated Press.*

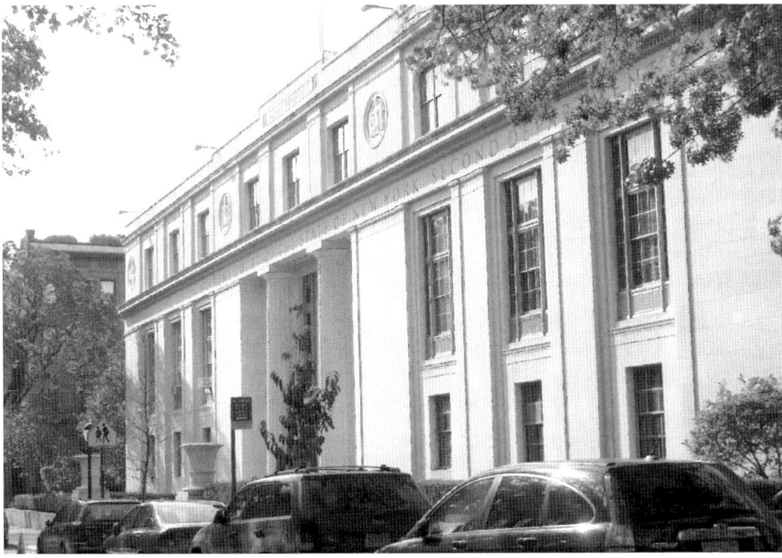

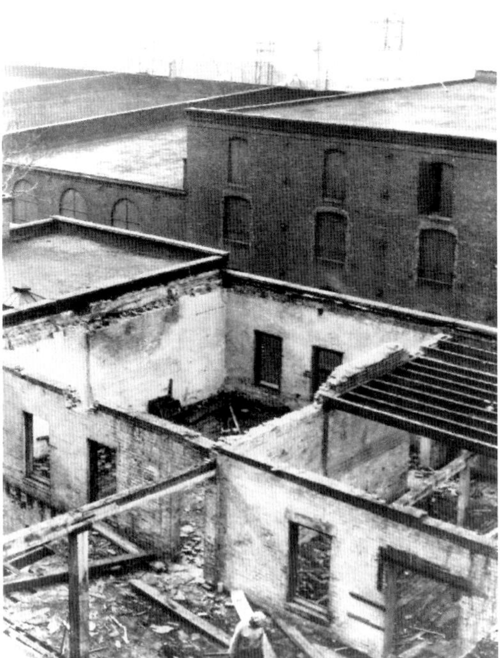

Above: An alarmed *Brooklyn Eagle* of September 19, 1942, ran the headline, "Plan for Express Highway Through Heights Is Shocking," and noted that the proposed route "would probably involve the demolition of the brand-new Appellate Division Court House, one of the most imposing buildings in the borough." Built in 1938 at Monroe Place and Pierrepont Street, the building is seen here in a November 2011 photograph.

Left: An early stage of warehouse demolition along the east side of Furman Street was recorded probably in late 1946. *Photo by Louise Casey.*

This only intensified efforts already begun by the Heights Association (not then yet referred to by its initials BHA) to work back channels for getting the route shifted to Furman Street.

Whether through the political influence that was brought to bear or—as the project's engineers later insisted was the case—because the potential condemnation costs for a Heights-bisecting route proved simply too great, the Furman Street route was settled on.

March 10, 1943

Now came the question of just how the highway along Furman would be built. When the one public hearing on the project was held, before the City Planning Commission on March 13, 1943—a time when the Great War was uppermost in all minds—the reporters present noted only that the highway route was unanimously supported. Short items in the *New York Times* and the *Brooklyn Eagle* missed entirely the significance of exchanges over the nature of the Furman Street section's design.

What was presented at the hearing was a highway essentially on one level (the outer lanes only two or three feet lower than the inner lanes) running behind the Columbia Heights houses. The transcript shows that Roy M.D. Richardson, a Wall Street corporate lawyer who was the Heights Association president, innocently alluded to people "promenading" along Columbia Heights whose views would be interfered with. Moses, a member of the planning commission, picked up on that word. This exchange was recorded:

> *Comm'r Moses: Where is the promenade you refer to on Brooklyn Heights?*
>
> *Mr. Richardson: It runs along Columbia Heights and there are parts at the intersecting streets.*
>
> *Comm'r Moses: You mean you can go to the street ends and look out from there, that is not a promenade.*

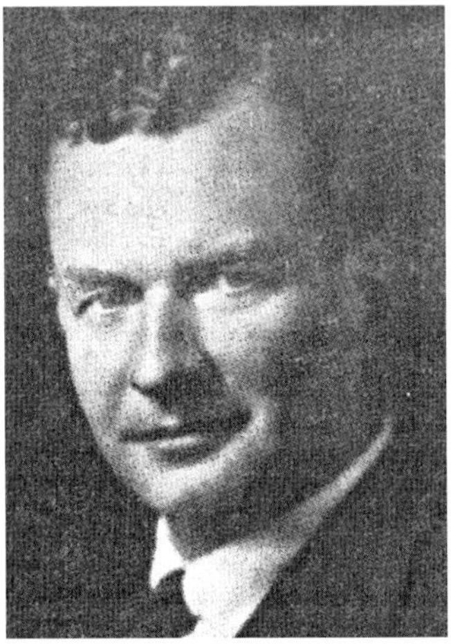

Left: Roy M.D. Richardson, as president of the Brooklyn Heights Association, worked to limit damage to the neighborhood posed by the planned highway. *Mrs. Roy Richardson.*

Below: Roy Richardson and his children posed behind their 218 Columbia Heights house in the winter of 1935–36. The snow-covered incline leading down to the roof of a Furman Street warehouse would give way late in the following decade to the concrete cantilevered structure that has the Promenade as its top. *Mrs. Roy Richardson.*

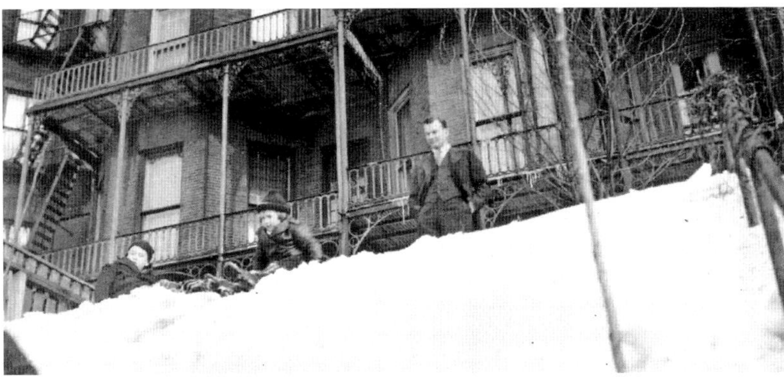

Mr. Richardson: Montague Street.

Comm'r Moses: That is not a promenade, either. A promenade is where you can walk for a certain distance.

Mr. Richardson: It is a matter of terminology.

Comm'r Moses: I think that is what the dictionary would say.

Mr. Richardson: I know those particular vistas are enjoyed by a great number of people.

Comm'r Moses: We think there should be more of them.

Now we know from minutes of Heights Association meetings and correspondence between Richardson and his neighbor several doors down Columbia Heights, Ferdinand ("Fred") Nitardy, a governor of the association, that there had been a hope that the highway could be built both lower and on separate decks. Nitardy, especially, hoped that it could also have a "cover" on which he could restore his splendid rear garden. (Richardson and Nitardy communicated at least several times by mail, addressing each other as "Dear Mr." with a formality that seems quaint today, but their surviving letters, preserved in Richardson's Brooklyn College library archive, are invaluable clues to the thinking that went on.)

Nitardy, the engineering vice-president in charge of construction for Squibb Pharmaceuticals, whose plant at the north end of Columbia Heights would later become the world administrative headquarters of Jehovah's Witnesses, spoke in down-to-earth tones that Moses reacted to with more sympathy than he accorded Richardson. The exchange between Moses and Nitardy (whose name the transcriber misspelled as "Miturdi") has Nitardy deferentially saying, "Naturally, I don't propose that I or my home shall stand in the way of progress for the Borough of Brooklyn," but then pleading that if it were possible

> *to make this street that would go on what is now private property a double-decker covered but opened toward Furman Street [to] make it possible to have the Highway just as you show it there and not do any damage whatsoever to the residential character of that property. The covering of the Highway toward the top but leaving it open toward Furman Street will cut out the annoyance of lights and noise of trucks and make it possible to retain the garden.*

After a couple of questions and answers with another commissioner, Moses interposed:

> *Comm'r Moses: I'd like to ask the gentleman a question, supposing that the Borough President and other authorities were willing, and*

> *I don't say I think they would be, to build this double-decker you speak of and there are lots of technical difficulties which probably we'll get into later, would you dedicate your land, assuming the City were willing to put a lot of dirt and grow some flowers on top of this double-decker and would your neighbors dedicate?*
>
> *Mr. Miturdi: I can't speak for my neighbors, but I will speak for myself. I will give the City free rights to this property so that the Highway is there.*

A little more followed before Moses concluded: "It is a very noble sentiment, but it wouldn't be shared by all the banks and lawyers who represent the other owners. I think you're in a class by yourself."

Moses's dismissive references to Nitardy's neighbors reflected an animus against the Heights that apparently had its roots in perhaps the most painful defeat of Moses's career: the blocking of his cherished plan for a majestic Brooklyn-Battery bridge, crossing the mouth of the East River to the southern tip of Manhattan. Moses had believed that the project was all set when, "[s]uddenly, on Wednesday, April 15, 1939, Mrs. Eleanor Roosevelt, in her 'My Day' column in the *New York World-Telegram*, leaped into the fray with her usual impetuosity," Moses wrote in his memoir *Public Works: A Dangerous Trade*. "She wrote, apparently at the instance of personal friends living on Brooklyn Heights," that the bridge would spoil beautiful views of Manhattan. The upshot was that Secretary of War Harry Woodring (the title was more honest in those days) in due course intervened, calling a bridge "eastward of a vital naval establishment [Brooklyn Navy Yard]" a potential enemy target and ordering that there instead be a tunnel, hidden from sight. Moses never got over that.

In addition to Richardson and Nitardy, a third Heights resident played a somewhat enigmatic role in this saga. That was Paul Windels, who, as the former city corporation counsel, had often been the intermediary in the prickly relationship between the imperious Moses and the fiery Mayor Fiorello LaGuardia. Windels was speaking at the close of the hearing when Moses brought up an earlier conversation.

Comm'r Moses: Some years ago you talked to some of us about a double-deck structure with cars running one way on an extension of Furman, an addition to Furman Street?

Mr. Windels: That must have been a good many years ago.

Comm'r Moses: Then the second level with the cars running in the second direction with a garden and esplanade on top. That always appealed to me.

"Aha!" I thought when I first read that; perhaps Moses was giving Windels credit for originating the idea of the Promenade! But no, wait a minute. Windels answered, "No, I don't recall ever having discussed through-traffic treatment with anyone," and he went on to explain that he was only concerned with keeping down the obstruction posed by the highway and wanted to "open up the area and make the great waterfront development." Many years later, his son, Paul Windels Jr., recalled to me how his father had taken him as a child down to the docks and talked of the possibility of creating there a great public space. So, evidently Paul Windels wasn't the genius behind the Promenade. Maybe he had the first vision for Brooklyn Bridge Park, which now in the twenty-first century is a 1.3-mile stretch of waterfront being transformed from its former use for merchant shipping into a green refuge?

In any event, these Heights people learned very soon that there would, in fact, be a double-decker with not private gardens but rather a public promenade on top. On April 13, 1943, four weeks after the cited hearing, Brooklyn Borough President John Cashmore (whose office technically had charge of the project) replied to Nitardy's renewed plea for restoration of his garden, writing: "I am obliged to say that the plan which we now have in mind would preclude the use by you of the deck of the two-storied highway which we propose to build. Instead of that, we have under consideration at the moment the adoption of a plan which would provide for an esplanade from Cranberry Street to or about Grace Court, similar in many respect, but I hope more attractive, than that portion of the east side drive which is in the neighborhood of Carl Schurz Park [i.e., at East Eighty-sixth Street, Manhattan]."

Also on the date of that letter, Richardson met with W. Earle Andrews, head of the engineering firm of Andrews and Clark, designers of the Furman Street section, and he followed it up with a letter objecting that "the promenade could not be sufficiently elevated to make the view a satisfactory one" (he wanted it kept as low as possible), unless, "of course, if the warehouses [across Furman Street] were torn down, there would be a grand view for all." (They would eventually be torn down.)

Nitardy kept on trying, noting in a letter to Richardson that "there is no need of a 50-ft.-wide promenade along Brooklyn Heights. The population of Brooklyn Heights is not such as to require such a wide promenade." Richardson joined in working for "grass and flowers"

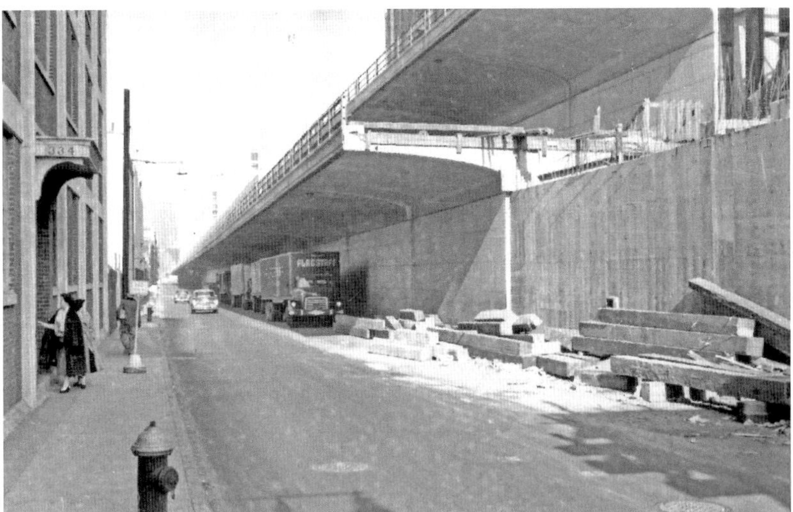

Above: Looking north on Furman Street from near Joralemon Street in November 1953, the lower deck of the BQE is still incomplete, although the Promenade (invisible above the second deck) has been in full use for almost two years. The BQE would not be ready for traffic until later in 1954.

Opposite: Louise Casey stands at the base of partly demolished warehouses on the east side of Furman Street, circa 1946–47. *Photo by Edward F. Casey.*

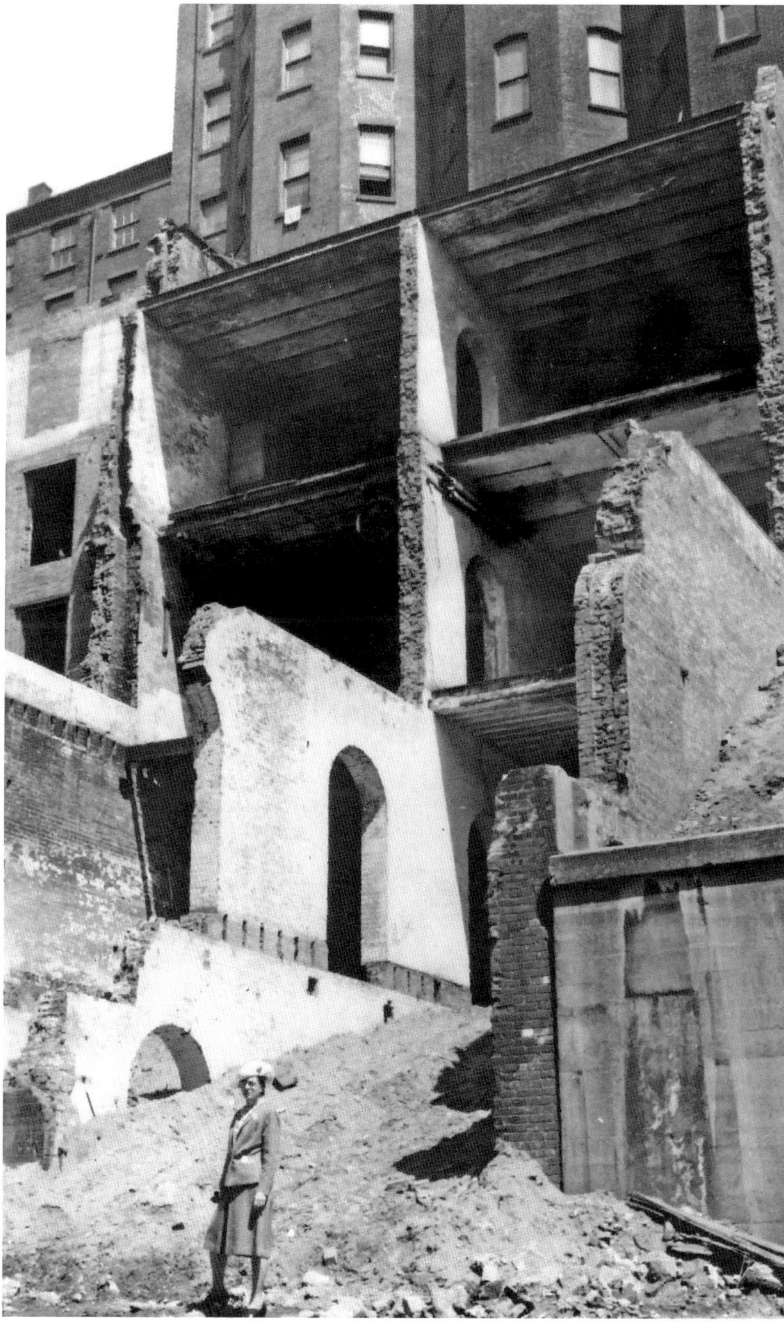

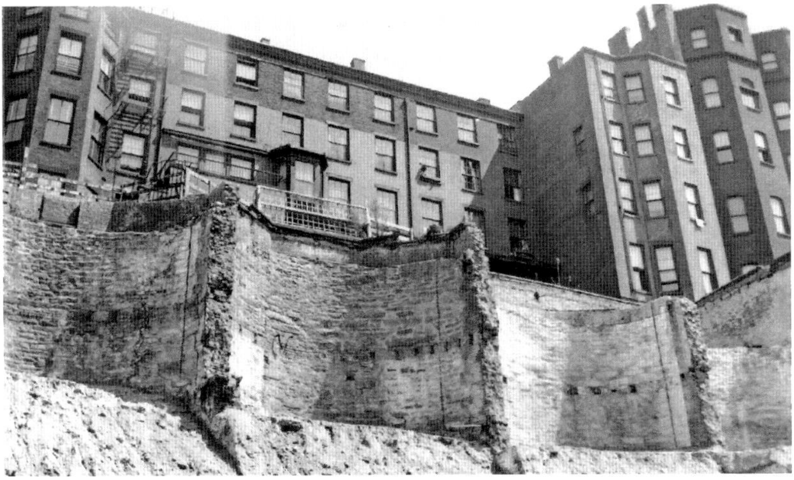

Massive vertical vaults show how the backs of the warehouses had been bolstered to act as retaining walls against the Brooklyn Heights embankment. This view probably dates to early 1947. *Photo by Louise Casey.*

to be planted on part of the deck, and he urged Heights residents and other Brooklyn organizations to write letters and make calls.

April 13 was also the date of a Heights Association meeting. The minutes of that meeting show reiterated support for a covered highway with the private gardens restored on top. No mention is made of a promenade. It is not until the minutes of the association's May 11 meeting that we find it summarized

> *that, in general, the City authorities have accepted the suggestions of the Association and are going to make a double decker, covered highway, taking, according to present plans, about 50 feet of the property along the Furman Street embankment. The highway will start being a double decker at Joralemon Street and there will be an esplanade on top of the highway, which will run from Grace Court to Middagh Street. There will probably be a strip of around 20 feet between the esplanade and the private residences.*

The funny thing about all of this is that Robert Moses surely knew ahead of the March 13 City Planning Commission hearing that the design for a promenade was well advanced. Drawings by Andrews and Clark found in the Richardson file, dated February 1943—the month *before* the hearing—clearly indicate the Promenade just as it would be built, running from Remsen Street to Orange Street, and with the circular endings at either terminus. For a plan that was supposedly not yet final, it had obviously had careful design attention. (Incidentally, the walkway is 25 feet wide along most of its length and 32 feet where there are bays of benches, and it is 1,850 feet long—a bit over one-third of a mile.) Was Moses just enjoying a little game with the Heights representatives at the hearing? Had Richardson not yet seen those February 1943 drawings? What did Cashmore really know? We can only surmise.

One unmistakable conclusion, though, is that the news of the Promenade sparked no jubilation at the Heights Association.

Claiming Credit

As with all successes, after the Promenade proved a hit, a number of people claimed at least a share of credit for it. One legend, which she evidently encouraged, had Gladys Underwood James telling Moses he had to run the highway along Furman and put a promenade on top. Mrs. James, the typewriter heiress whose carefully selected investments in Heights brownstones were the effective first steps toward the district's historic preservation, had a close connection to Moses in that her-father-in-law had given Moses his first job out of Yale. Moses was sometimes a guest at her house, but in a letter to me he denied that she had influenced the project, and there is serious question as to when and where she might have done her persuading. Her name does not come up in the Richardson correspondence or the Heights Association documents.

B. Meredith Langstaff, a leading Heights activist and author of the Heights Association–sponsored history *Brooklyn Heights: Yesterday—Today—Tomorrow* (1937), told me in 1981: "I rushed there to Moses and told him we must not have a highway through the Heights, and he stopped it. I suggested the plan that is there now of having two things hanging out from the Heights." Langstaff wasn't known for shyness about his claims to fame.

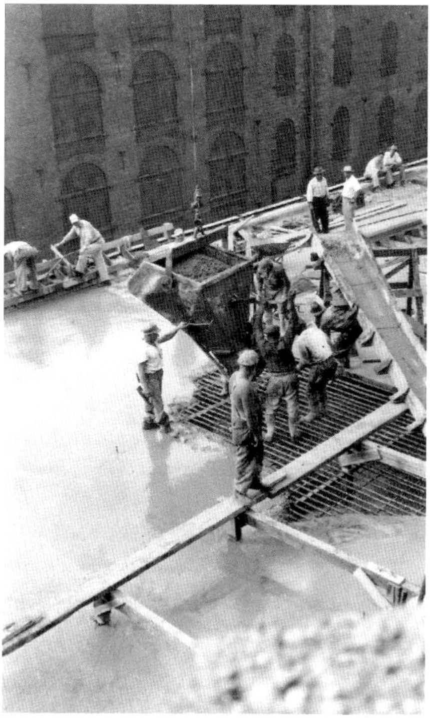

Concrete is laid on the upper traffic deck of the BQE in September 1948. *Photo by Louise Casey.*

Although the evidence overwhelmingly points to the engineers at Andrews and Clark as having carried out the cantilever design, the distinguished landscape engineering firm of Clarke and Rapuano made the drawings for the gardens along the Promenade, and some within that firm believed Michael Rapuano had actually conceived of the cantilever. Their argument was that no one at Andrews and Clark matched him for experience and design brilliance. But they couldn't supply proof.

Easily the most detailed claim for credit came from an Andrews and Clark engineer named S. Starr Walbridge, who wrote to me in 1982, saying, "It was soley [*sic*] my idea to use cantilevers to support Brooklyn Queens Expressway along Columbia Heights, and it was soley my idea to have a cantilevered pedestrian walk, or promenade, above the upper road." Walbridge went on to describe how he had discussed with Julian Michele, the artist who did the firm's renderings, how the highway decks should be supported and urged him to show them as cantilevers instead of carried on columns or stilts. Walbridge supplied a great deal of other information about the cantilever and the Promenade's construction. But when I called Michele for corroboration, he refused to comment on Walbridge's claim other than to say, "We were all good friends at the time, and I hate to think we're old and cranky now and turning nasty."

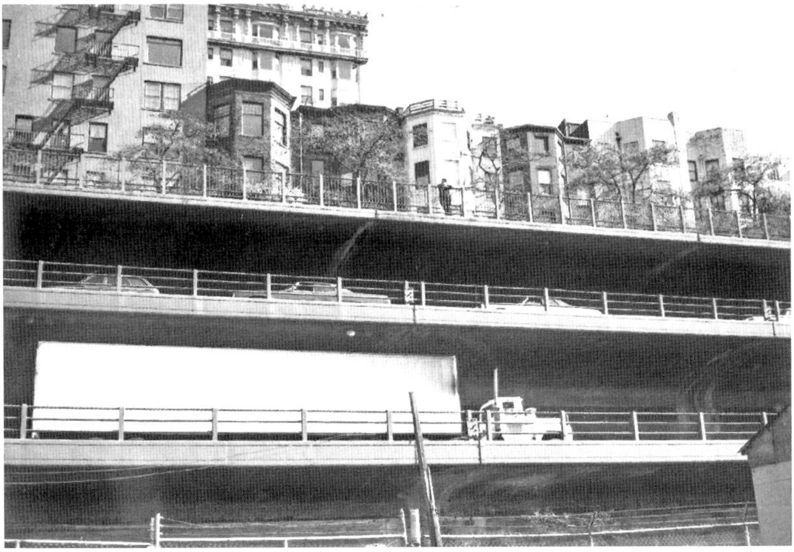

Trucks much bigger than what existed at the time of the BQE's planning, like this one seen in 1981, have tested the cantilever's strength and durability.

Walbridge's claim was also challenged by other surviving members of the firm. (The one who could have known for sure, W. Earle Andrews, had died long before my inquiries.) Ernest J. Clark, the project's chief engineer, insisted that the design had been arrived at through trial and error by the team's collaborative effort. Different ways of supporting the roadways had been considered and their stresses and looks tested. As Clark recounted it, the cantilever design had *evolved*.

One team member who was acknowledged as executing the actual engineering design of the cantilever structure was Phillips H. Lovering, who, in an unsigned article for the May 27, 1948 *Engineering News-Record*, explained, "The undersides of the cantilevers, although appearing parabolic, are actually quadrants of ellipses so designed as to prevent the sound of highway traffic from being focused on the dock structures on Furman St., and reflected back and upward to become a continual nuisance to the residents on Columbia Heights." (With the subsequent demolition of those warehouses, this design precaution was rendered unnecessary; how it might affect visitors on Brooklyn Bridge Park is a different question.)

A man who made no undue claims for himself, the Brooklyn-born Lovering, in a letter to me from his island home in Puget Sound in 1982, mentioned a surprising fact about the head of the Del Balso construction company that built the cantilever: "Our resident engineer frequently went to lunch with Mr. Del Balso who always said he had left his glasses in the office and asked what was on the menu. Our resident engineer told us it took him considerable time to discover that Mr. Del Balso was illiterate. Of

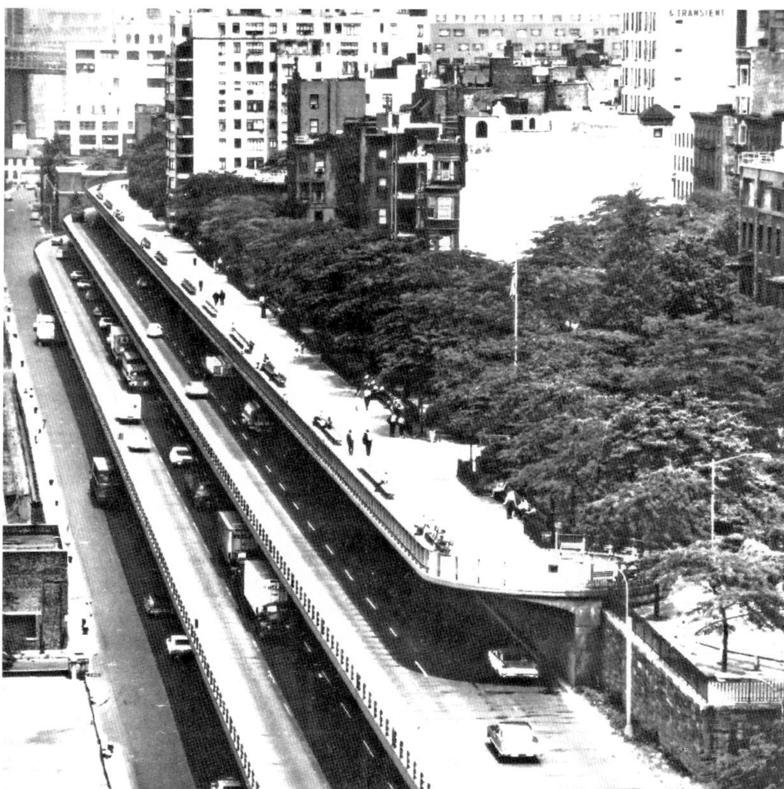

This Andrews and Clark aerial photograph of the Promenade section of the Brooklyn-Queens Expressway was made no earlier than 1954, the year the BQE was opened to vehicular traffic.

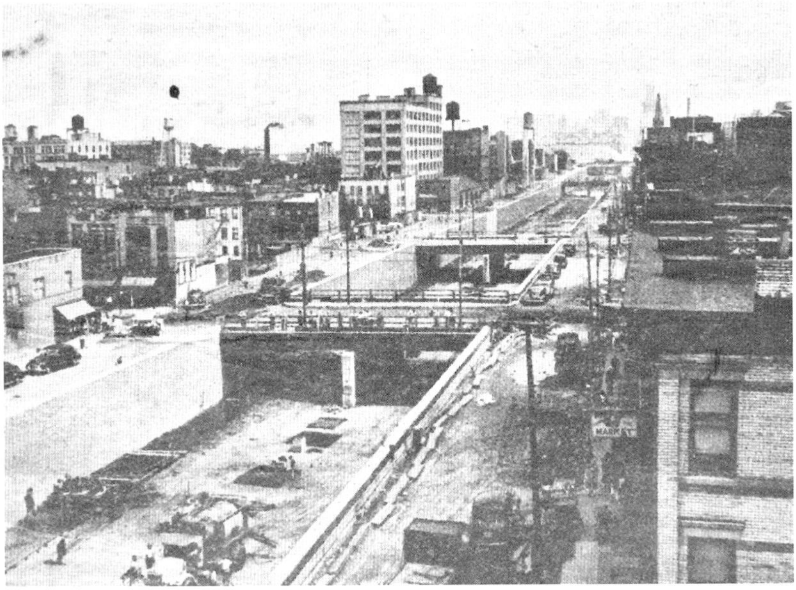

South of Atlantic Avenue, there was no community organization that could counter Robert Moses, with the result that part of the Brooklyn-Queens Expressway was built in a cut along Hicks Street, the hated "ditch" of the area now known as Cobble Hill. This photo of its construction, probably from 1948, is taken from prior publication in the *Brooklyn Heights Press*, since the Triborough Bridge and Tunnel Authority, from which the original print had been borrowed and then returned, could not locate it in response to a subsequent request.

course he had his own engineer and I think his son so that the plans were faithfully followed."

Lovering's design was forwarded to an engineer named Shortridge Hardesty, whom Walbridge described as "the consultant's consultant." Hardesty found that the design could carry the projected loads but recommended some additional stiffening to prevent any vibration that might make drivers uneasy. We no doubt have Hardesty to thank for the fact that the highway (which did not open until 1954, well after the Promenade) has survived for fifty-seven years at this writing while carrying eighteen-wheeler trucks far heavier than any in use at the time of the design.

The Promenade Gets Built

The actual construction of what became known as the Brooklyn-Queens Expressway, or BQE, as well as its Promenade section, had to wait until after the end of the war. Demolition of the warehouses along the east side of Furman Street began in late 1946, and the Montague Street cut leading to the docks began to be partly filled in, requiring elimination of its traversing sweet little Penny Bridge and the arched viewing platform that also had straddled the cut.

Impatience joined apprehension as construction slowly proceeded. "The promenade, so far, has been a nightmare to people living in those [Columbia Heights] houses: promenaders peering into windows of homes, and hoodlums shouting in unseemly language," wrote columnist Margaret Mara in the February 24, 1950 *Brooklyn Eagle*. "The wall bounding the promenade on the street has been convenient for the intruders peering into windows." She called for regular police patrols.

"The work has been dragging on for years," J.G. Black complained in a letter to the June 19, 1950 *Eagle*. The letter noted that the Promenade "is completely fenced in, cutting off the view at Remsen, Montague and Pierrepont Streets."

"By the time the project is put to use," Black continued, "the iron railing over on the river side will probably be a streak of rust."

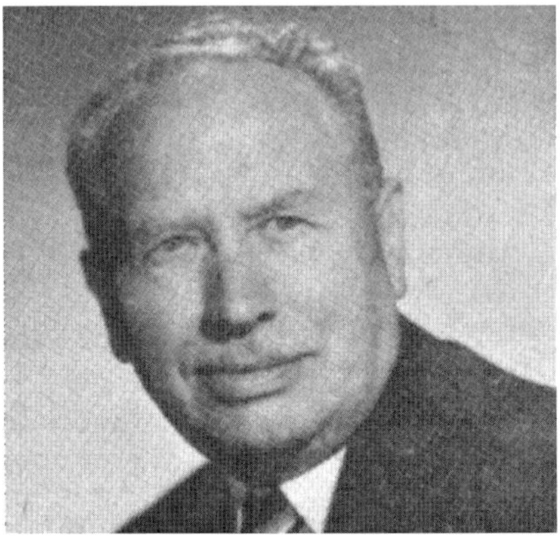

Ferdinand ("Fred") Nitardy argued for a "cover" on the planned highway on which he could restore his prized rear garden. *The Nitardy family.*

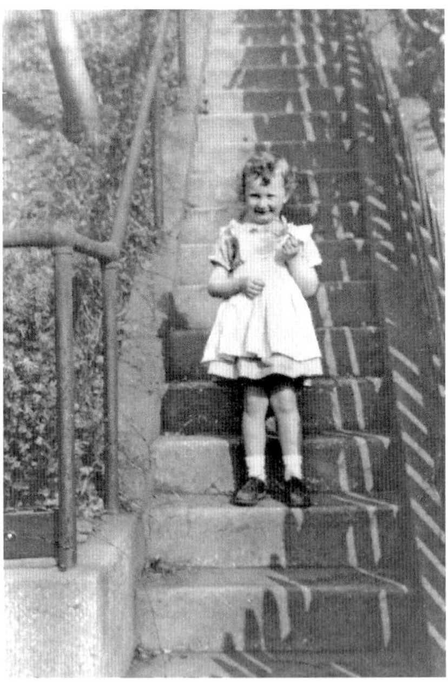

Janet ("Jill") Richardson stood in the spring of 1940 on the steps leading from the family's upper garden to the one on the warehouse roof below. *Mrs. Roy Richardson.*

The continual pile driving had also gotten on people's nerves. "I remember the regular beat of it," Mrs. Edward P. Beach recalled to me, "*boomp boomp boomp.*" And she mentioned the time that "we almost slid into the bay one night. The whole bank began crumbling."

That danger passed, but in 1949, information that honey locust trees would be planted in the twenty-foot-wide Promenade garden strip at twenty- to twenty-four-foot intervals disturbed Nitardy and Richardson. Richardson, now the association's ex-president, wrote to Moses saying that trees potentially reaching a height of sixty feet meant that "what is left of our gardens [could be] thrown into almost perpetual shade." However, the trees went in.

By the time the ceremonial opening the first Promenade section, the portion south of Clark Street, took place on October 8, 1950, most of the worries had quickly dissipated. The immediate popularity of the Promenade led to an even bigger ceremony the following year, when, on December 7, 1951 (the tenth

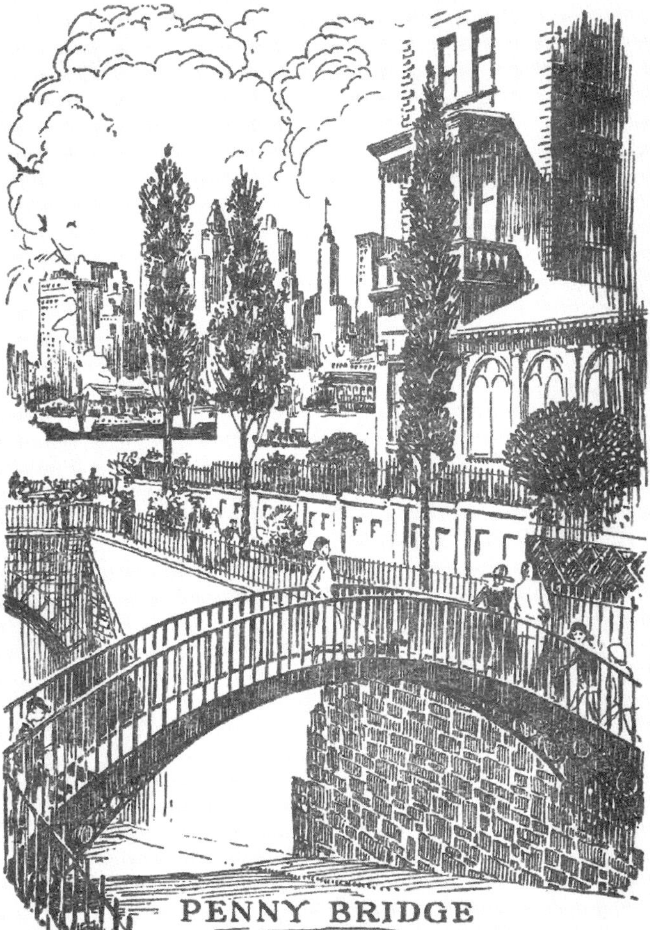

BROOKLYN HEIGHTS

The fondly remembered little Penny Bridge straddled the Montague Street cut near its start, providing a pedestrian link between two one-block streets, Pierrepont Place and Montague Terrace. Also straddling the cut a short distance farther down, a viewing platform built of stone was the chief public place from which to view harbor and skyline before the Promenade replaced it. This drawing is from a real estate promotion sent out by the long-defunct Cary, Harmon Corporation in 1952, by which time the Penny Bridge was gone and the Promenade was in full use.

anniversary of Pearl Harbor), the remaining section was opened. Borough President Cashmore hailed Robert Moses as the Leonardo da Vinci of his day. One small sour note: Roy Richardson's widow told me many years later that Richardson had not been invited to that ceremony.

Whether invited or not, Nitardy would undoubtedly have shunned the ceremony. "Father of the Promenade" in the eyes of a number of fellow Heights residents, he was apparently never reconciled to the form it took. Certainly Mrs. Nitardy wasn't. Long after her husband's death, she fulminated against the Promenade and the strangers walking on it who peered into what remained of her garden. The other member of the Heights trio, Paul Windels, did not live on Columbia Heights and so he experienced no direct personal consequence of the Promenade's existence.

The Heights Association soon warmed to the Promenade and before long took a proprietary role in the care of its gardens (and even implied a more direct role in the Promenade's creation), though it objected to the popular name and hewed to the more genteel "Esplanade." With the passing of the generation that had been at best ambivalent about so public an attraction in that sedate neighborhood, the insistence on "esplanade" diminished. When Henry J. Stern—the 1990s commissioner of parks and recreation who delighted in giving names to public spaces without city council or other authorization—had signs reading "Brooklyn Heights Promenade" placed at its entrances, that effectively ended the name game.

The Promenade became not only a place for locals and tourists to stroll and enjoy the magnificent view south, west and north, but it also drew joggers, bicyclists (not legally permitted), nannies pushing baby conveyances and those just looking for a place to relax or keep an amorous tryst. For some years, semiannual art shows were held there, until complaints that they had degenerated into mere kitsch- and trinket-selling affairs led to their curtailment. Huge crowds requiring police cordons were drawn to Fourth of July evening fireworks displays in the East River sponsored by Macy's department stores (but not in 2010, when the fireworks were set off on the Hudson River). Not infrequently, Promenade visitors

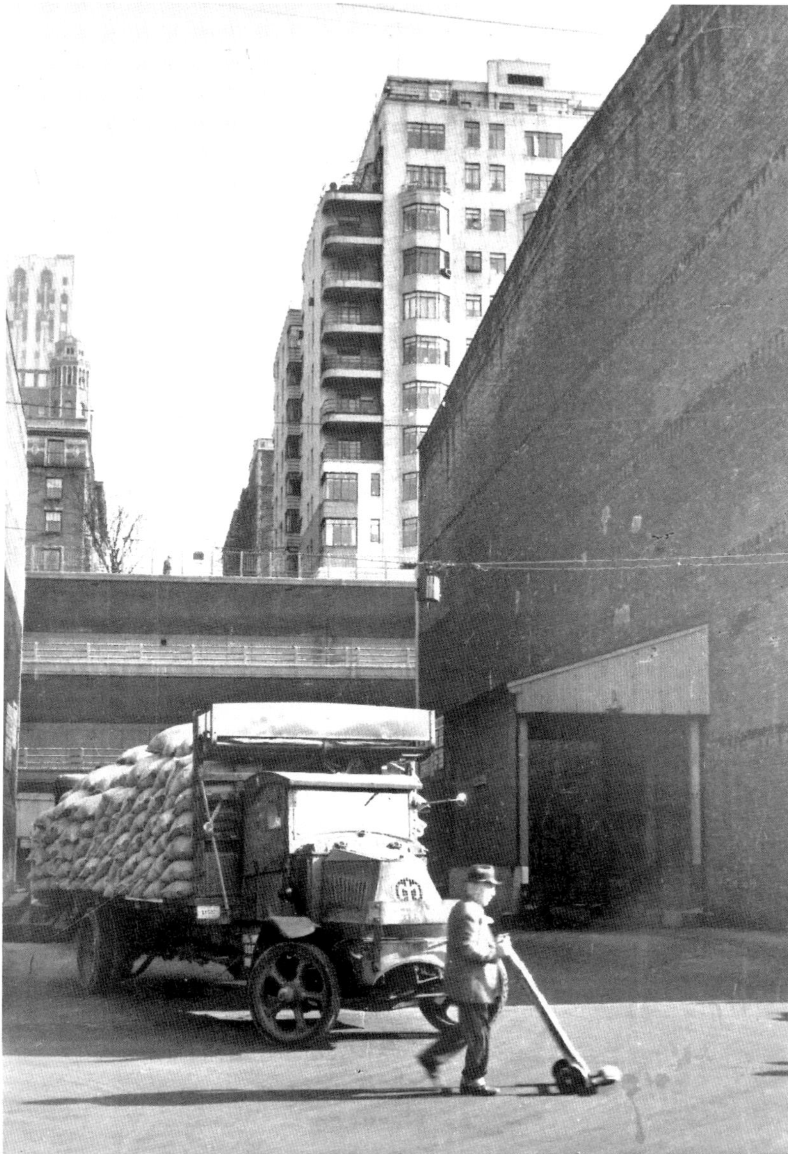

A longshoreman pushes a hand truck by the docks below Clark Street in 1953. The Promenade and BQE are visible beyond the grain-carrying truck. Above looms the apartment house at 160 Columbia Heights. The warehouse at right and other warehouses along the west side of Furman Street were torn down later in the decade.

have also been treated to unadvertised fireworks celebrating some private anniversary or occasion. The babble of tongues heard on the Promenade even includes English.

Many a bride and groom have posed on the Promenade for their wedding albums. Rather touchingly, Robert Moses wrote to me late in his long life that he understood that the Promenade was much used for professional photography and movie scenes, though he had not personally witnessed this.

A Threat Survived

The expressway hadn't even opened when in the spring of April 1953 there arose a threat to the Promenade. The Port of New York Authority (now the Port Authority of New York and New Jersey), under whose jurisdiction fell the four-story warehouses that limited views from the Promenade (which was fifty feet above Furman Street), wanted to reserve the right to replace them with seventy-foot structures. The local furor led to a rare "town hall" meeting at Borough Hall, where Borough President Cashmore, Moses and other officials temporized. When I wrote to Moses questioning his apparent indifference, he surprisingly wrote back at some length, pointing out a number of complications and contending that "[t]he City cannot do a piece of spot zoning simply protecting this particular view."

Remarkably enough, after an interim fifty-foot "Class S" zoning district was approved later that year, and after the warehouses were torn down in the late 1950s, "spot zoning" was precisely what got enacted through the city's first "Special Scenic District" for the Promenade in 1974. This established a "view plane" from the edge of the Promenade to roughly the middle of the East River above which no structures could rise. That zoning protects the view to this day.

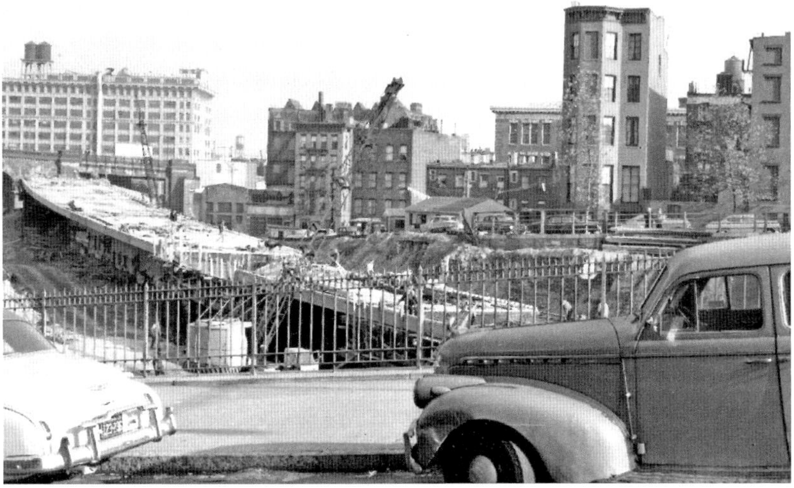

North of Middagh Street, the highway, still under construction, is seen veering eastward in November 1953. While the Furman Street route had meant a big savings in condemnation costs compared to a Heights-bisecting route, some significant houses were lost where the highway began its swing, including the Columbia Heights house from which the physically disabled Washington Roebling had overseen construction of the Brooklyn Bridge and the "writers' house" on Middagh Street where W.H. Auden, Carson McCullers and others had lived for a time. Where the highway took up land that had been covered by rear gardens, modest condemnation sums were paid.

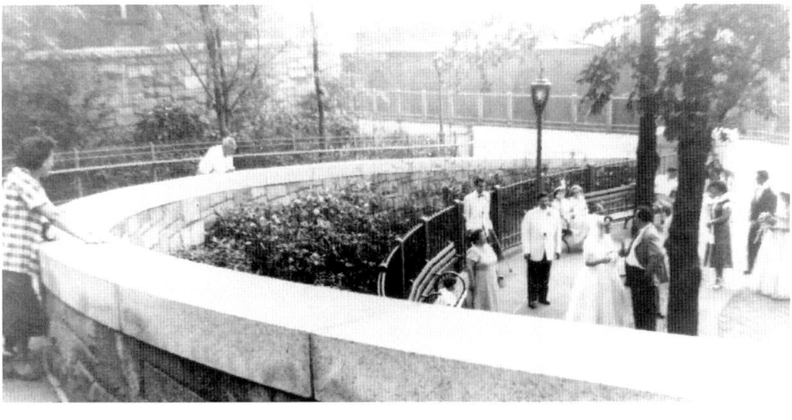

It wasn't long before the Promenade caught on as a site for weddings and for photographs of many family and social occasions. This wedding took place at the Promenade's northern, Orange Street circle in May 1953. Warehouses still lined the opposite side of Furman Street.

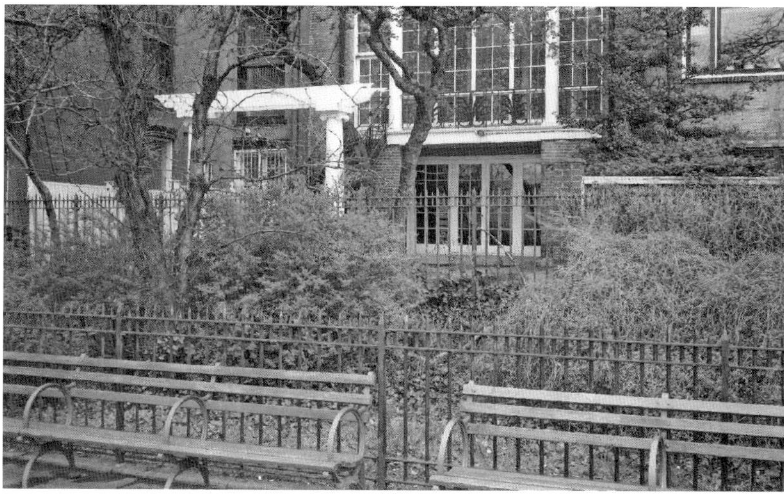

The truncated Nitardy garden behind 176 Columbia Heights in April 1985, with the Promenade's rear fence and park benches set against it. The level of their garden was closer to that of the Promenade than many others along Columbia Heights. Fred Nitardy and his wife never reconciled themselves to the Promenade's existence.

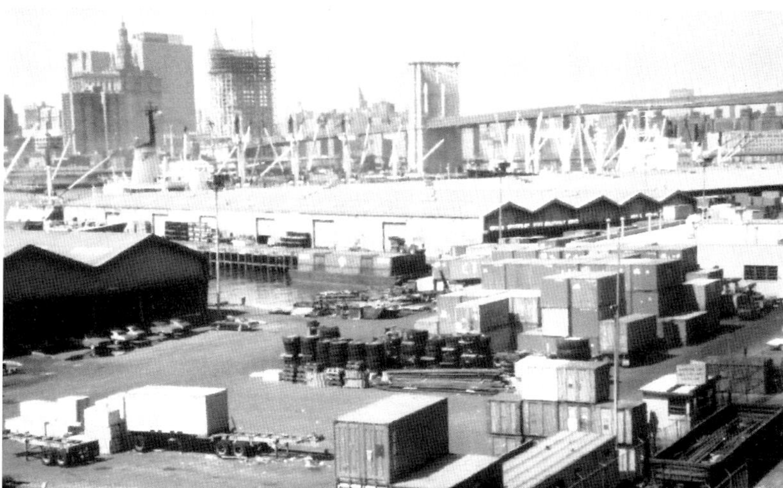

After containers began replacing what was known as break-bulk cargo, the piers below the Heights remained active for about another decade, until the ships specifically designed to carry containers grew so large that the piers and the upland no longer sufficed to service them. Here, containers stood between Piers 1 and 2 in April 1974 awaiting further disposition.

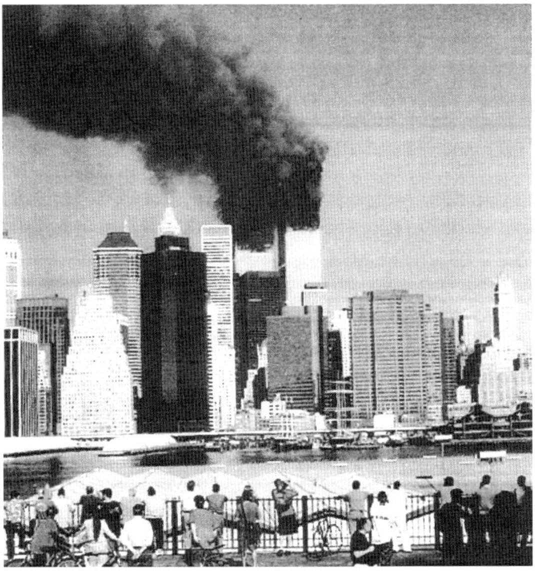

Left: New York City's darkest moment drew many to the Promenade to observe the devastation, as the towers of the World Trade Center went up in smoke following the terrorist attack of September 11, 2001. *Photo by Don Evans,* Brooklyn Eagle.

Opposite, top: With smoke still hovering over Lower Manhattan the day after the September 11 attack, sorrowful people came to the Promenade to mourn and reflect.

Opposite, middle: In the days and weeks that followed, memorial tributes of all sorts were placed along the Promenade, and the base of the flagpole at the Montague Street entrance became an informal shrine, as seen here on September 20, 2001.

Opposite, bottom: A photograph of the Manhattan skyline with the World Trade Center towers at its center was installed anonymously on the Promenade's fence soon after the attack, and it has remained there undisturbed through the years. This photo was taken in April 2011 as the tenth anniversary of the attack was approaching.

As for the view, it afforded much foreground interest as long as the docks were alive with shipping. After the space demands of containerization basically shut down the piers by late 1984, only a rare ship was seen there, and until serious work on Brooklyn Bridge Park began for that stretch in 2009–2010, the pier sheds were mostly vacant and desolate. (Some cocoa and coffee imports were stored in a couple of them, and for a time, Pier 3 was occupied by a supplier of lumber and building materials.) At this writing, the

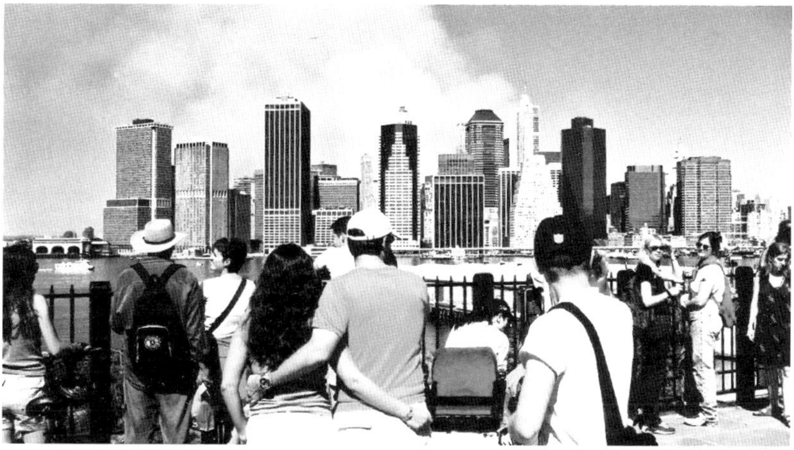

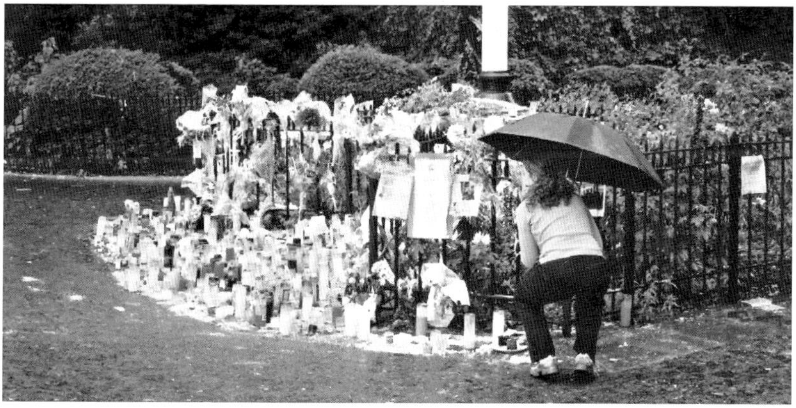

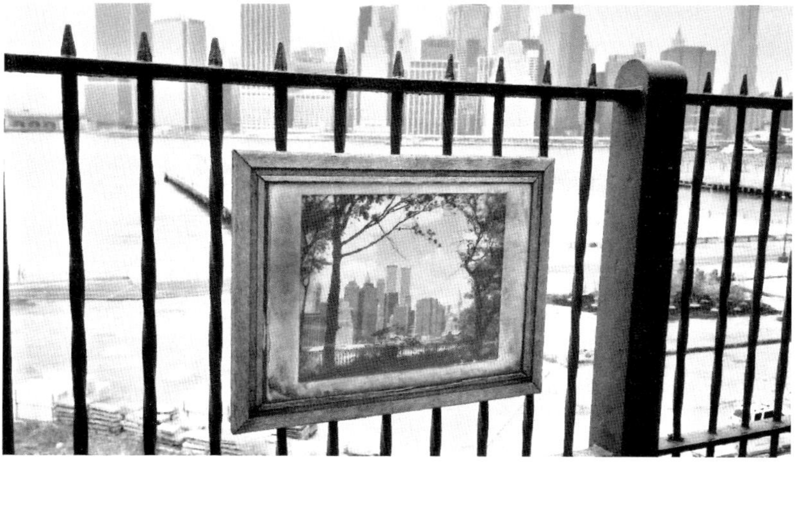

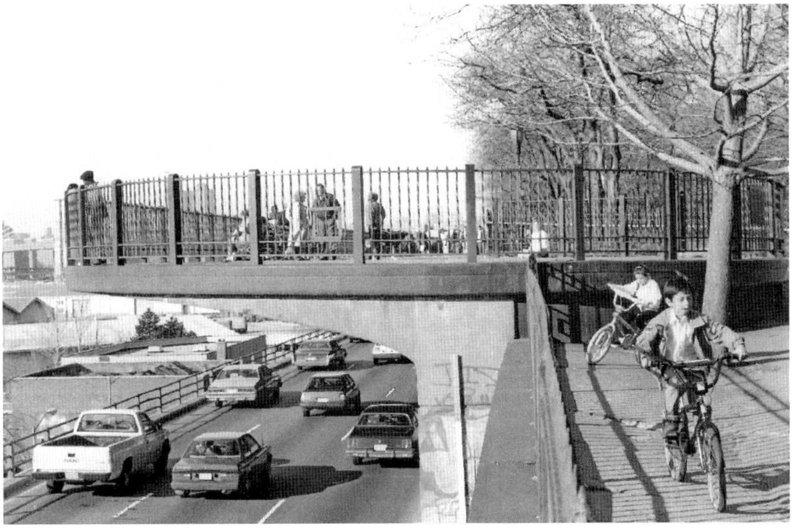

The projection of the Heights Promenade above the northbound traffic deck of the Brooklyn-Queens Expressway is clearly shown in this 1991 view from the foot of Remsen Street, where two boys are riding bicycles.

platforms of Piers 2, 3 and 5 are still bare, but park development has been taking place on their landward sides. (Pier 4, which had been privately owned, has been left to deteriorate, becoming an ever diminishing remnant that is hoped to keep attracting birds and sea life.) When the park is finally completed, the view of the foreground will compete with the harbor, skyline and bridges beyond.

Whatever happens to the now aging highway and its unusual cantilever segment (will the BQE be rerouted or even placed in a tunnel?), the Promenade appears sure to remain in place, although needing repair. It has become too integral a part of Brooklyn Heights, and too important a draw for visitors—a venerated landmark, in short—to be allowed to disappear.

Part II

The Promenade through the Years: Selected Newspaper Excerpts

"How We Almost Lost the View from the Promenade"

Brooklyn Heights Press, May 13, 1976

New York City offers spectacular views to the person with an office or apartment high in the sky. Those who can't afford the rent aren't so lucky. But there is one place where a supreme view—perhaps the finest in the city—has easy public access, and that is the view of the downtown skyline and the harbor from the Brooklyn Heights Promenade.

The Promenade is unique in the city and must be counted among the marvels of the world.

When it was formally opened to strollers on Saturday, October 7, 1950, the event was relatively little noted. The *Herald-Tribune* reported that two hundred persons turned out for the ribbon-cutting ceremony at the foot of Montague Street, where the speakers included Acting Mayor Vincent R. Impelliteri, Borough President John Cashmore and Park Commissioner Robert Moses.

The *Trib*, which gave the story four paragraphs...said Cashmore gave major credit for the planning of the Promenade to Philip P. Farley, who was chief consulting engineer in the borough president's office.

The idea of girdling Brooklyn Heights with two elevated highway levels was the kind of vision that passed for bold in its time—to accomplish it meant having to defeat a prior plan that would have sent the Brooklyn-Queens Expressway thundering down a vastly widened Hicks Street—but to put in a top deck simply for the enjoyment of people on foot was so radical that it almost escaped notice.

While Robert Moses claimed credit at least for being "one of those who originally suggested the Esplanade on the three-story expressway system," he did not find it worth remarking on in his book, "Public Works: A Dangerous Trade," though the book does contain a photograph of the three cantilevered levels, with this caption, quoted in its entirety: "Brooklyn-Queens Expressway in Brooklyn showing two-level road with promenade above overlooking East River and Lower Manhattan." The Promenade doesn't rate even that much mention from Robert A. Caro in his massive critical biography of Moses, "The Power Broker."

The oversight may be explained by a post–World War II mentality that couldn't recognize the Promenade as a big deal because it didn't move cars. That mentality may also help explain how it could happen that, two-and-a-half years after the Promenade was completed, we came in danger of losing its magnificent view.

Between the docks and Furman Street, below the Promenade, was a row of old warehouses, most of which did not reach the fifty-foot height of the Promenade. The Port Authority and the New York Dock Company wanted to be free to replace those warehouses with 70-foot structures, which would have blocked the view.

In a day when most environmental protest was feeble, a rollicking fight ensued. The Brooklyn Heights Association distributed leaflets. Bank and real estate people and—in the words of the *Brooklyn Eagle*—"rank-and-file residents" took part in rallies and wrote letters and signed petitions.

A special "town hall" meeting brought an overflow crowd to Borough Hall, where Borough President Cashmore shared the podium with Robert Moses and representatives of the Port Authority and other agencies. Ostensibly Cashmore sided with the protesters, but he gave a curious performance, as did Moses. It seemed there were many complicated questions regarding zoning regulations. For some reason it was not possible to establish a zone for the Brooklyn Heights section of the waterfront that did not apply to the entire waterfront. Moses talked about exploring aerial easements, but he conveyed no sense of commitment to trying to save the view. Cashmore's remarks were couched in impenetrable, legalistic bureaucratese.

People in the crowd tried vainly to pin them down on where they stood. One polite gentleman who had received an evasive answer from Cashmore tried painfully to rephrase his question, only to be evaded again.

"Mr. Cashmore, what he wants to know is are you for us or agin' us?" That question, from my mother in a deliberately colloquial affectation, brought down the house. There was momentary consternation on the podium, but when the meeting settled down again, Cashmore's assurance that of course he was for us came mixed with a lecture that we didn't understand the complexities involved.

The next day, May 8, 1953, the *Brooklyn Eagle* reported the meeting under the headline "Cashmore Backed in Bid to Keep 50-Foot Limit on Dock Buildings." The way the story read, one would have thought Cashmore had been trying to rally his followers in a course of defiance instead of having done his successful best to avoid a single solid word of commitment.

Cashmore was, of course, a very small cog compared to Robert Moses, who was then City Construction Co-Ordinator and a City Planning Commissioner, as well as chairman of the Triborough Bridge and New York City Tunnel Authorities, City Park Commissioner, head of the Mayor's Slum Clearance Committee, member of the City Traffic Commission and a consultant in various areas at federal, state and county levels and, on occasion, to foreign governments. I'm sure I've left some posts out.

I wrote a letter to Moses, saying I was surprised by his apparent lack of position on the issue. To my further surprise, I got a two-page reply, not a form letter, single-spaced and with narrow margins on large sheets of stationery, dictated and signed by him.

"Dear Lieutenant," it began. (I was then in the U.S. Air Force, on temporary duty assignment away from the Air Force psychological warfare center, which was in Mountain Home, Idaho, of all places—

but that's an altogether different story—and in those days it might have looked unpatriotic if a public official didn't reply to a concerned service man.) Much of the letter contained the kind of obfuscation we had heard at Borough Hall, although Moses did claim, "From the very beginning, I have urged protection of the view," and, "Without attempting to claim undue credit I think you will find that as a matter of historic fact I was one of those who originally suggested the Esplanade on the three-story expressway system."

He added that it had been built over "enormous opposition" by "property owners who didn't want their back yards taken and bitterly opposed having the common run of folks use this walk."

But Moses stressed that "Frankly I don't think you have sufficiently studied the problem of zoning on the Heights…enough to understand it completely…" He included a sentence I just did not believe was true: "The city cannot do a piece of spot zoning simply protecting this particular view."

I wrote Moses again and got a shorter reply that included the sentence: "The notion that the height below seventy-feet at the waterfront would be measured from the eyes of a person on a [*sic*] Esplanade is just too silly for words."

Meanwhile, the Brooklyn Heights Association renewed its efforts, circulating an appeal for a letter-writing campaign, but, in apparent acceptance of the idea that esthetics was then an all but un-American defense, the association urged letter-writers to soft-pedal the matter of the view and concentrate instead on the "health hazard" posed by 70-foot buildings. The association had determined that noxious fumes from the expressway would bounce off the building walls and cause imminent danger to the health of the nearby residents.

Strangely enough, Port Authority Executive Director Austin Tobin had himself suggested he would be agreeable to a zoning amendment that specified a height of 70 feet "but in no instance higher than a public esplanade." In his second letter to me, Moses remarked, "I have very little confidence in any new amendment incorporating the curious suggestions made by my friend Austin Tobin."

What Moses was after I have no idea to this day. I can't believe he wanted to destroy the view from the Promenade, which after all, couldn't have been built without his support—if not initiation.

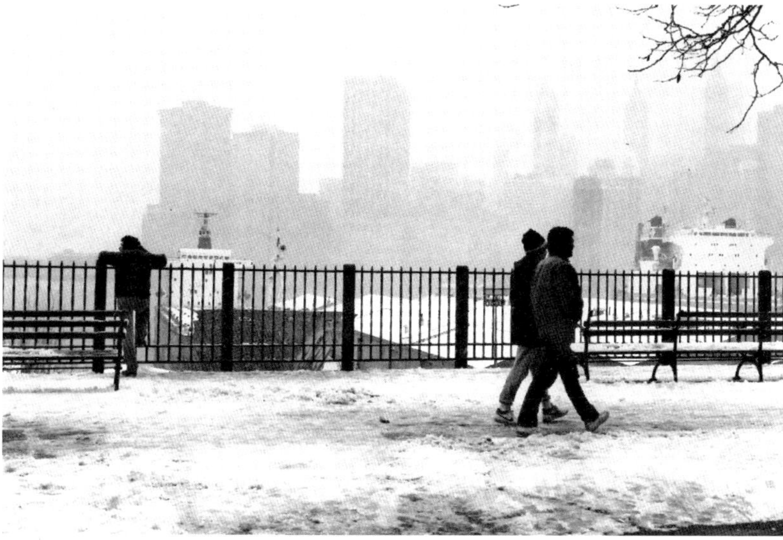

Some people can be found on the Promenade in almost any kind of weather. In this February 1985 instance, icy snow and slush did not keep these promenaders away. The ships at the piers were by then obsolete containerships (already too small) awaiting mothballing and demolition elsewhere.

Known as he was for his power and arrogance, why did he trouble to attend the Borough Hall meeting? Why did he personally answer two letters from an obscure Air Force lieutenant? I can only think he was hedging on the zoning matter out of some consideration that never came to light and that, from Moses' point of view, never needed to.

For, as it turned out, on June 25, 1953, the Board of Estimate approved a 50-foot limit for the Brooklyn Heights waterfront, and, above its prepared lead story on the subject, the *Brooklyn Heights Press* had time to insert a one-paragraph bulletin that the view was safe.

Since then, most of the old warehouses have been torn down and not replaced by new dock buildings. The result is a much more complete view today: you can see the freighters at the piers and far more of the harbor. I only wish that the 1953 skyline had not been flattened by all those skyscraper boxes of the 1960's.

"Looking Back on the Heights: A Promenade for All Seasons, A Supreme Urban Vantage Point"

Brooklyn Heights Press and Cobble Hill News, January 26, 1978

The Brooklyn Heights Promenade came about as an afterthought. When it had been built, we almost lost the great view it opened up to us. It remains all but ignored in the accounts of Robert Moses, whose afterthought it appears to have been, and without whom it would not have been built.

Nobody planned the Promenade.

As you stroll along it on an afternoon, enjoying its expansive panorama of ships, docks, water, skyscrapers and sky—while trying to steer clear of illegal bicycles, dogs or (any day now) snowmobiles—consider that this magnificent pedestrian way was the near-accidental result of compromise in the face of public opposition to what had been planned originally.

Today, of course, no project of any size gets carried out without prior screening by more-or-less representative community groups; but the Promenade was built in the Era of Moses, when community wishes counted for little.

That may be a reason Robert Moses has never made too much of the Promenade when listing his achievements (in his book, "Public Works: A Dangerous Trade," it is mentioned only in a picture caption; and his critic Robert Caro makes no mention of it at all in

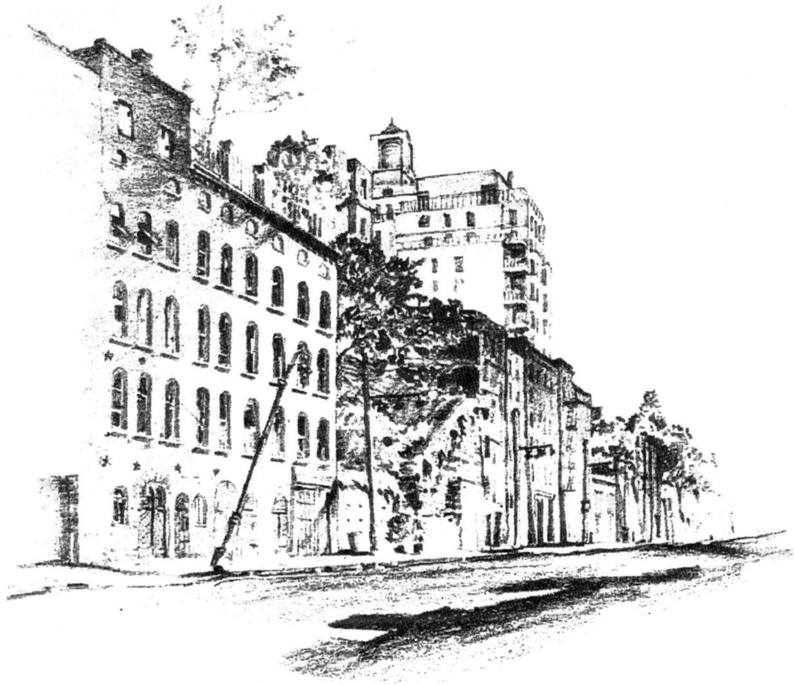

Near the northern end of Furman Street, warehouses lined the east side of the street and the west, and a steep stairway provided dockworkers with a link to the Heights. In this sketch, presumably by Julian Michele, the apartment building above is 160 Columbia Heights. *From an Andrews and Clark brochure.*

"The Power Broker: Robert Moses and the Fall of New York"). Still, at the Oct. 7, 1950 ceremony that marked the official opening of the first section of the Promenade, Moses did say: "I don't know of anything quite like this in any city of the world."

There are cities with rival waterside views. I've never been on Avenida Atlantica at the Copacabana in Rio de Janeiro, but I have been at the banks of the Seine in Paris, the Grand Canal in Venice, the Golden Horn in Istanbul, Marine Drive in Bombay, the ghats of Banaras, the klongs of Bangkok, the Nile at Luxor, the Embarcadero in San Francisco. The view from the Heights Promenade is as soul-satisfying as any of these. One could argue that it offers the supreme urban prospect.

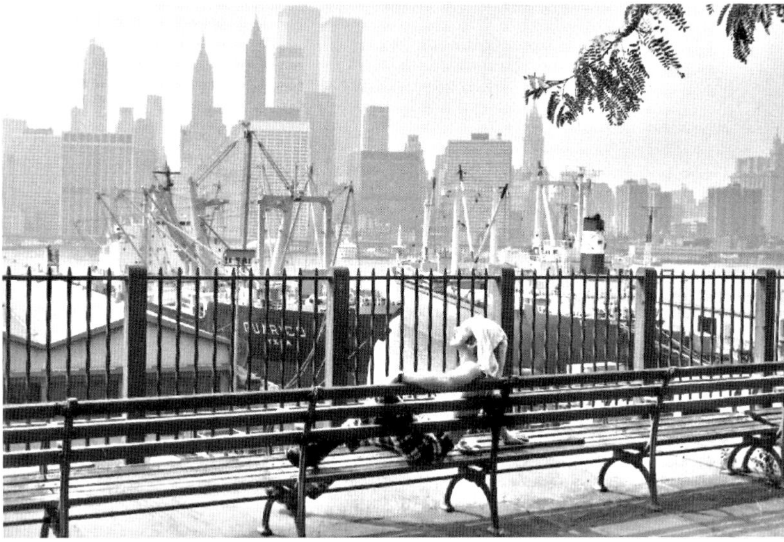

A man found some relief on the Promenade from a heat wave in July 1977. Elimination of the warehouses two decades earlier had opened up views of the freighters docked below.

(As my mother from time to time has observed, people who insist on living in Manhattan fail to appreciate that no view from Manhattan is equal to the view of Manhattan from Brooklyn.)

Often, before I turn in at night, I feel the need to take one final look from the Promenade. Sometimes, in icy weather that keeps most people away from the stinging gusts, the Promenade presents its most jewel-like glimpses of the skyline and harbor. Hung with heat in July, it can drive away all but the most determined sunbathers. In the summer haze and glare, the Promenade may not be at its best; even so, a brief detour along there can help dispel the accumulated mental clutter of "one who has been long in city pent."

On the whole, I've always preferred the Promenade in its less crowded moments. I recall an evening's passionate embrace with a girl named Brewer in the shadows near 160 Columbia Heights, even though her first name escapes me—I only know it wasn't Theresa, which was the name of a popular singer at the time. I can recall other times when I was alone and lonely, and being mysteriously soothed by the sight of freighters docked and smaller craft moving busily in the East River and lights playing on the water.

For an older generation the Promenade has served—perhaps still serves—as a place for summoning up memories of a yet earlier New York. For instance, in the "Old Timers" column of the June 21, 1958 issue of the *World Telegram* contributor James A. Mannix wrote: "You are seated on a bench of the Heights Promenade. You look across the harbor and you see Ellis Island and the Manhattan skyline. What memories come to you!

"Recall when Werner's Express handled the immigrants who came through Ellis Island? Remember the once famous wireless office there, from which many old-time ship news reporters covered the arrival of ships?"

Ship news reporters? They were once front page stuff. Today you find them, if at all, back near the day's television listings in the *Times*. Or at least that's where you could sometimes find ship news before the *Times* came up with all those "Living" and other weekday sections.

Now the harbor is less crowded. Ships are still there, but the thought arises: did the completion of the Promenade almost precisely at mid-century coincide with the then as yet unrecognized beginning of the decline of New York?

It's a troubling thought, and we'll push it aside for now.

The other side—perhaps the more living side—of the Promenade is as stage for a human pageant against the backdrop of harbor and skyline. This can be vivid enough to make one wish we had our own Canaletto to record the scene. It's never quite as sedate as our more sedate residents might wish it to be.

The dogs, bicyclists, the joggers—skiers even—infiltrate the pageant. One Saturday afternoon, when my then five-year-old son was just learning to ride a two-wheeler down by the foot of Pierrepont Street, he suddenly veered off onto the Promenade and struck an old lady a glancing blow. For a moment I envisioned my life undone by a million-dollar lawsuit. Luckily, she wasn't harmed.

The most incongruous spectacle is the outdoor art show that seems in recent years to have been returning to the Promenade with increasing frequency. The art on display is invariably of a quality so inferior to that splendor of its setting that one wonders if the makers of such work have any sensibility at all.

It would be too much to call the Promenade itself a work of art. Its railings, benches, walkway tiles are no more than serviceable—the uninspired serviceability that marks the Moses style.

The inspiration was not in the execution but in the idea that this unparalleled setting could be used for a pedestrian deck above two decks designed for automobiles—which, in the Moses scheme of things, were what really counted. One has only to remember that a decade later Robert Moses successfully fought off all suggestions for a pedestrian way on the Verrazano Narrows Bridge.

How did the Promenade come about?

The first plan for the Brooklyn Heights section of the Brooklyn-Queens Expressway called for "a curved diagonal cut through the Heights from Atlantic Avenue and Hicks Street to Tillary and Washington Streets. This plan, which would have cut the Heights in two, was vigorously opposed by the [Brooklyn Heights] Association."

That quotation is taken from an unsigned column, "The Old Timer Writes," in the *Brooklyn Heights Press*, April 9, 1953. The column goes on to say that the City Planning Commission (of which Robert Moses was officially only a member) next proposed an elevated 6-lane highway "at the level of the present promenade, on top of the embankment east of Furman Street directly under the residences on the west side of Columbia Heights."

At a March, 1945 meeting of the Heights Association, an alternative plan for a covered multi-level highway was agreed on, according to the column, and the next day members of the Association brought that suggestion before a Planning Commission hearing; but they had little hope of success, inasmuch as the Brooklyn Chamber of Commerce, the Downtown Civil Council and other Brooklyn organizations all favored the City Planning Commission's proposal.

When all seemed lost, the Old Timer wrote, "A Brooklyn Heights Association member then asked for permission to speak as an interested property owner."

Now here's a curious note. The Old Timer concluded his column with the observation: "Names of residents have been omitted from this article because their modesty is opposed to disclosure of the roles they played in the establishment of the Esplanade."

So, for the moment, let it be an anonymous Heights Association member who, "Addressing himself particularly to Mr. Moses, he stated…much of the damage [to Columbia Heights properties] could be avoided by a double deck covered highway, built into the embankment…

"Mr. Moses seemed impressed, and…said he would agree to have the proposal studied, but…he would prefer to see the cover used for a public promenade, instead of having it revert to private gardens."

Right there, the Promenade seems to have been born. Two months later, the City Planning Commission approved the promenade concept.

Who was the anonymous speaker? His name had already appeared in the *Heights Press*, and his identity was otherwise no secret. In a column of September 27, 1951, called "Ye Olde Breucklen Heights," T.A. Gorman had written: "At a meeting in City Hall, Mr. F.W. Nitardy, a landholder of Columbia Heights, recommended that a double deck roadway with a cover over it be adopted as the plan. Mr. Nitardy stated that he and other property owners along the proposed right of way would give the city a portion of their backyard gardens which faced the harbor, if the gardens could be replaced by the city on top of the cover above the proposed highway."

About the time all this was going on, I used to play stickball with boys, among whom was Mr. Nitardy's son Walter. In my eyes, Walter was an outfielder on a par with Dixie Walker of the Brooklyn Dodgers. He could foil a sure extra-base hit by darting between parked cars and leaping off their fenders for the catch. He could also hit the ball a block. (Where have all the stickball players gone? Vanished, like the Dodgers.)

All I knew about Mr. Nitardy was that he was a vice president of Squibb, back when that pharmaceutical company instead of Jehovah's Witnesses occupied the buildings near the Fulton Ferry end of Columbia Heights. It seems he was also a vice president of the Brooklyn Heights Association.

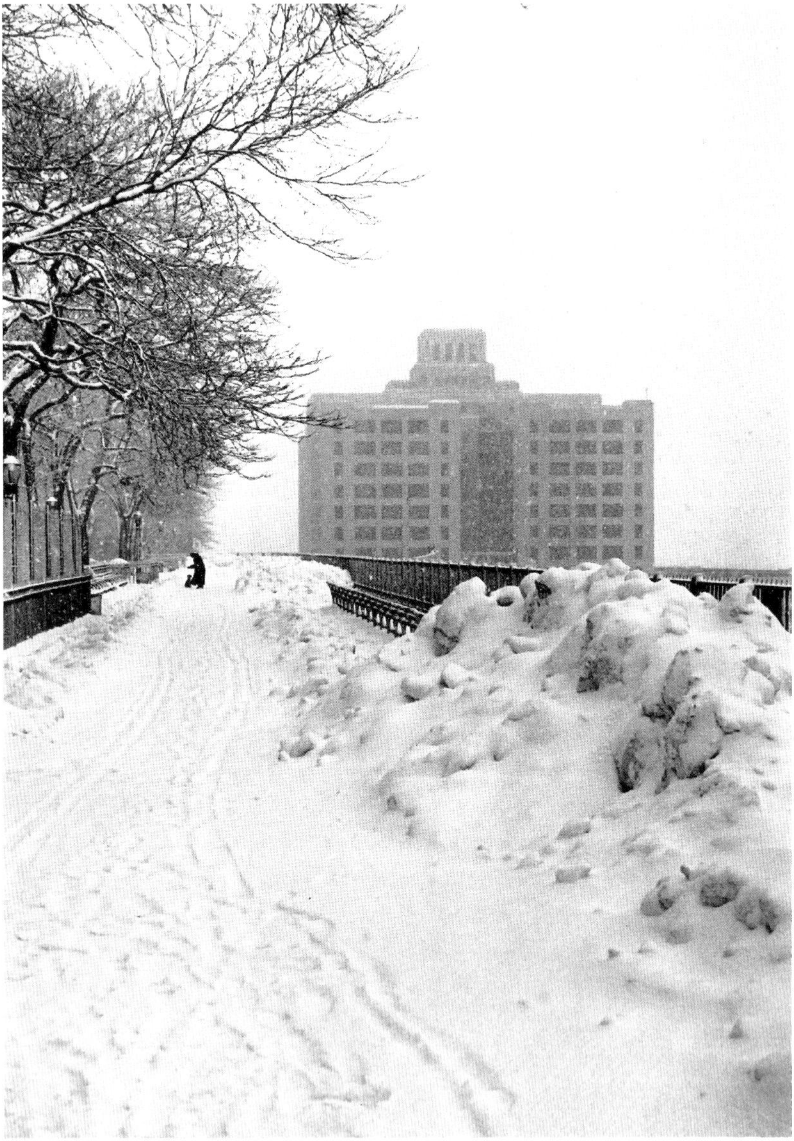

A second snowfall in January 1996 that covered piles left from a previous big storm didn't deter the woman in the distance from walking her dog on the Promenade. The building in the background, 360 Furman Street, had been sold by the New York Dock Company to Jehovah's Witnesses, who used it for a packaging plant and other services before in turn selling it in the new millennium for conversion into apartments with the new name of One Brooklyn Bridge Park.

In those days I wasn't aware of the struggle over the Brooklyn-Queens Expressway, and I was only vaguely aware that some people were unhappy even after construction began.

Going through clippings at the Long Island Historical Society the other day, I came across this from the "Living in Brooklyn" column of Margaret Mara in the February 24, 1950 *Brooklyn Eagle*: "The Promenade, so far, has been a nightmare for people living in those houses; promenaders peering into windows of homes and hoodlums shouting in unseemly language."

The same year, in the June 19 issue of the *Eagle*, letter-writer J.G. Black complained: "As for the promenade, it is entirely fenced in, cutting off the view at Remsen, Montague, and Pierrepont Streets." He wrote that "the work has been dragging on for years" and pleaded that the Promenade be opened to the public. He had not quite four more months to wait.

To this day one can hear of Columbia Heights residents who aren't fully reconciled to their backyards not culminating in a public walk. But on the whole the Promenade must be accounted an overwhelming success.

And yet, while that success was evident from the day the first section opened (the stretch from Remsen Street to Clark Street), it wasn't long before the city—with what looked like passive concurrence on the part of Robert Moses—almost allowed the view from the Promenade to be destroyed.

The Port Authority was considering replacing the old warehouses along Furman Street with new buildings that would have reached higher than the Promenade, blocking the view. A whole new fight ensued, in which Mr. Nitardy once again played a leading role.

By then I was out of college and in the Air Force, and was beginning to take an interest in civic matters. I wrote letters, and I treasure two replies to "Dear Lieutenant" from Robert Moses in his capacity as City Construction Co-Ordinator, in which he explained at some length how difficult it would be to establish and justify a special zoning district to protect the view.

While, in a letter of May 11, 1953, Moses observed, "I think you will find as a matter of historic fact that I was one of those who originally suggested the Esplanade," in a second reply to me just one week later he wrote: "The notion that the height below seventy-feet at the waterfront would be measured from the eyes of a person on a [*sic*] Esplanade is just too silly for words."

Among those who had opposed zoning protection for the Promenade view were the Brooklyn Chamber of Commerce and the Brooklyn Real Estate Board. A somewhat reluctant champion of those who wanted the view protected was Borough President John Cashmore, who, at a Board of Estimate meeting had "pointed out that the city has a $7,500,000 investment in the Promenade and should be willing to take measures to protect its investment." (BHP, July 24, 1952.)

One June 24, 1953, with Cashmore having cashed his political chips, the Board of Estimate approved a special "Class S" zone for the Heights, and the Promenade view was safe. (A fuller account of some events in this latter struggle can be found in my article, "How We Almost Lost the View from the Promenade," BHP, May 13, 1976.)

Robert Moses rightly deserves credit in that he, finally, seems to have been the one who saw the chance to give the general public a view that previously had belonged only to privileged homeowners and tenants. But Moses has never given it proper place among his accomplishments, and if he fought for it when it was later in danger, his public behavior would not tend to bear this out.

Perhaps Moses was too proud to claim excessive credit for what was only an afterthought. Perhaps the fact that the Promenade came about by way of compromise with angered citizens made it seem less glorious than a project carried out as conceived, in the face of opposition.

In any event, there it is: the Brooklyn Heights Promenade, a magnificent creation of inadvertence, a triumph for pedestrians and aesthetics rather than automobile drivers or commerce, an achievement never properly appreciated except by the public that came to enjoy it.

It just can't be that the completion of the Promenade at mid-century can have borne any relation to the beginning of the decline of New York!

"The Promenade: Origins of a Miracle in Urban Design"

Brooklyn Heights Press and Cobble Hill News, February 8, 1979

While the Heights Press lays no claim to the comprehensiveness of a newspaper of record, in matters of the surprisingly obscure history of the Heights Promenade it has become an indispensable source. To fans of the Promenade, therefore, we owe an update and correction as to the course and timing of certain events that helped bring this miracle of urban design into being.

Marina Yu, a graduate student of urban planning at Columbia University, has forwarded to us a paper in which she expanded on the research made previously by this writer.

Although her conclusion in no way disputes our earlier assertion that "Nobody planned the Promenade" (BHP, Jan. 26, 1978), she finds that the key developments came earlier than we had believed.

The Promenade, in a sense, took everyone by surprise, and the significance of the events leading to its construction seems to have struck people only afterwards, by which time faulty memories and perhaps typographical errors came into play.

From the files of the Heights Press, an unsigned column by "The Old Timer," April 9, 1953, recalls that the Brooklyn Heights section of the Brooklyn-Queens Expressway was first intended to follow "a curved diagonal cut through the Heights from Atlantic Avenue and

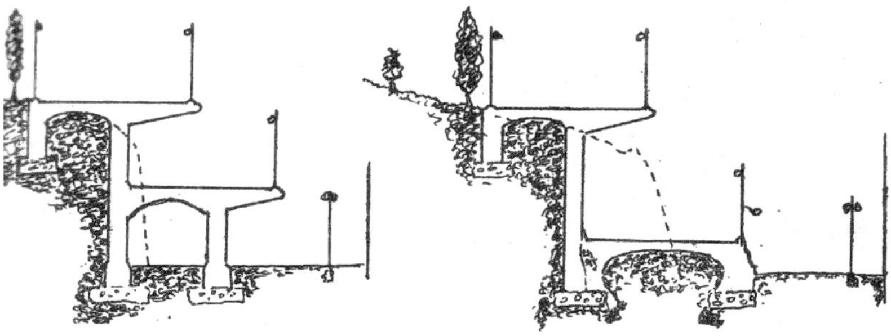

Fred Tuemmler of the City Planning Department had anticipated a cantilevered construction as part of a "special treatment" of a highway section along Brooklyn Heights. In these 1939 sketches, he indicated a split-level highway jutting out from the bluffs of the Heights. However, the idea of an additional promenade level was not part of his proposal. The sketches were included in Tuemmler's "A Proposal for a Brooklyn-Queens East River Highway," issued January 30, 1940. *Avery Library, Columbia University.*

Hicks Street to Tillary and Washington Streets. This plan, which would have cut the Heights in two, was vigorously opposed by the [Brooklyn Heights] Association."

However, Ms. Yu looked up the original Master Plan proposal by the Department of City Planning, January 1940, and found it recommended that the Heights section be a two-level highway above Furman Street, with the possibility of running the upper traffic deck along the cliffs of Columbia Heights, approximately where the Promenade is now.

The "diagonal cut" mentioned by the Old Timer was, Ms. Yu reports, one of several alternatives that subsequently came out of the office of Borough President John Cashmere, who was most interested in trying to "upgrade and revitalize the Brooklyn Civic Center."

"Not surprisingly," Ms. Yu writes, "this [diagonal cut] plan met with vigorous opposition by the Board of Governors of the Brooklyn Heights Association which received notification of the plan in October 1942."

In any event, the city preferred the Furman Street route—but with a six-lane deck along the edge of Columbia Heights. The Downtown Brooklyn Association, the Brooklyn Real Estate Board, the Brooklyn Chamber of Commerce, the Borough President's office—all but the Brooklyn Heights Association and local residents—agreed with that plan.

The crucial moment came at a City Planning Commission hearing, which, Ms. Yu points out, took place—not in March 1945, as our files have it, but on March 10, 1943.

For the substance of what happened there, Ms. Yu has had to rely, as did we previously, on the recollections of our Old Timer, who described how, when all seemed lost, Columbia Heights property owner Ferdinand W. Nitardy was called on to speak. Aiming his remarks particularly at the powerful Robert Moses, the late Mr. Nitardy argued for a "double deck covered highway built into the embankment instead of on top of it, that it would require the taking of less private property and further, he would give the City free right of way through his own property, as would several of his neighbors, with whom he had discussed the matter, if the City would then put the then existing gardens back on the cover.

"Mr. Moses seemed impressed," the Old Timer's account continues, "and after some questions, said he would agree to have the proposal studied, but in case it proved feasible, he would prefer to see the cover for a public promenade, instead of having it revert to private gardens."

In May 1943, the City Planning Commission approved the covered highway idea.

Queries to Deputy City Comptroller Paul M. O'Brien, who was editor of the Heights Press in 1952–54 when the "Old Timer" column appeared, as well as to others, have failed to elicit any recollection of the Old Timer's identity. (A very similar account of the Planning Commission hearing, though slightly less detailed, was given by the late Thomas A. Gorman in his column, "Ye Olde Breucklen Heights," BHP, Sept. 27, 1951.)

The question of who designed the Promenade, once it was decided upon, has no clear answer. Ms. Yu writes:

"Responsibility for the actual design of the Promenade appears to have been a collaborative effort among the engineers employed in the office of the Brooklyn Borough President, the private engineering consulting firm of Andrews, Clark and Buckley (later renamed Andrews and Clark) and the City Planning Department. When the Promenade was formally opened on October 7, 1950 (though it was not completed until a year after), at the ceremony, Brooklyn Borough President Cashmore, of course, gave major credit for the planning and design of the Promenade to Philip Farley, chief engineer in his office. On the other hand, the *A.I.A. Guide to New York City* gives credit to Fred Tuemmler of the City Planning Department for having 'created one of the few brilliant solutions for the relationship of automobile, pedestrian and city.' (However, the only reference to F. Tuemmler I came across were in connection with arterial maps proposed for the Master Plan crediting him with responsibility for the mapping.) The firm Andrews and Clark, however, claims credit for having done the actual designing of the Promenade and the Furman Street section of the Brooklyn-Queens Expressway."

By the way, the original 1967 edition of the *A.I.A. Guide* makes no mention of Tuemmler; that reference was added to the 1968 edition.

"Saving" the Promenade

In the 1960s, while Lincoln Center was still in the later stages of construction, humorist Art Buchwald wrote a column: "Save Lincoln Center!" During that last frenzy of the construction boom, they seemed to be tearing Manhattan down faster even than they were rebuilding it.

Buchwald's caution was not entirely farfetched. One only needs to see what nearly happened to the Heights Promenade not long after the final section was opened on December 7, 1951. In "How We Almost Lost the View from the Promenade" (BHP, May 13, 1976), this writer recounted how community action—at a time when that had not yet become fashionable—staved off the threat

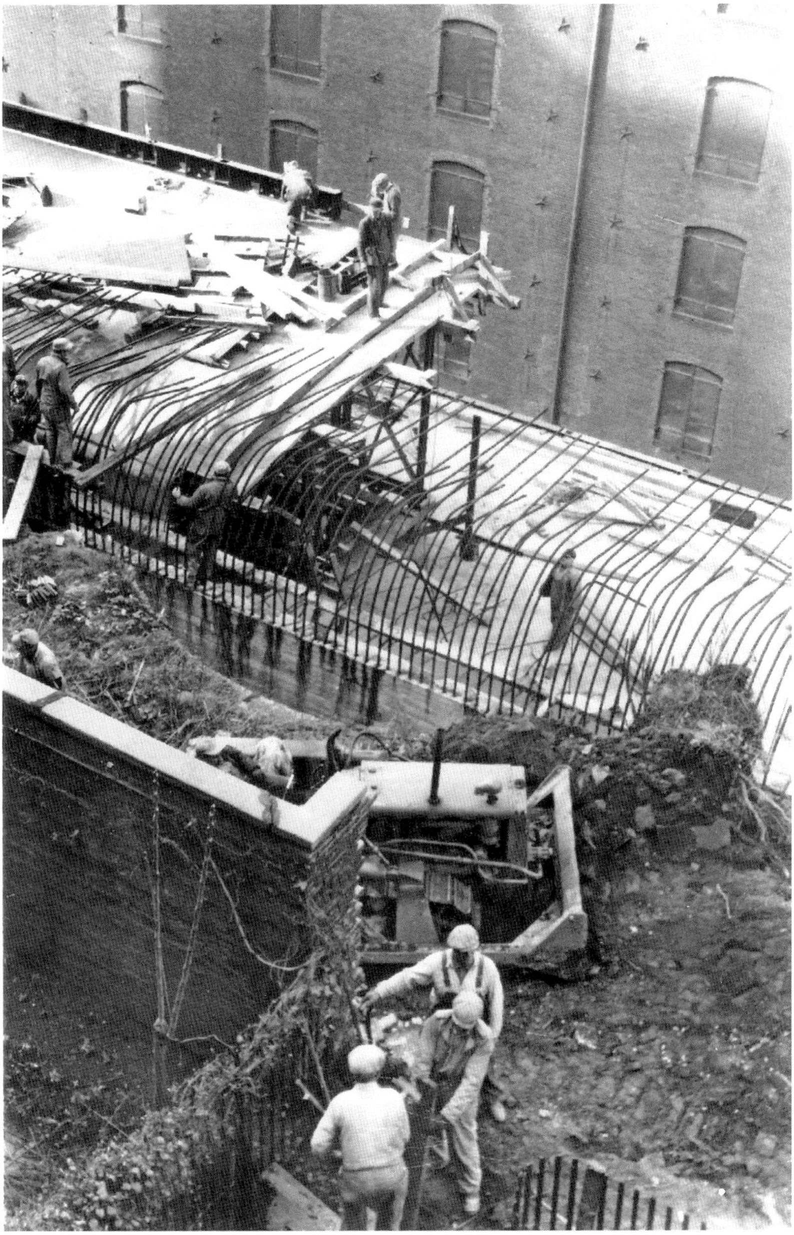

In this undated photograph, two traffic decks are progressing, while the future Promenade is indicated by bent reinforcing rods. *Photo by Louise Casey.*

of pier buildings rising across Furman Street to a height that would have blocked the Promenade's view.

Robert Moses was curiously indifferent to that threat, evidently not taking the same pride in the Promenade that he might have in a project more deeply involving his own vision of what should be. After all, he had suggested the Promenade only as an afterthought and by way of compromise to get on with the larger project, the Brooklyn-Queens Expressway (larger to him, anyway).

As it turned out, with Ferdinand Nitardy again playing a leading role (he was a vice president of the Squibb Corporation, and, at this juncture, also vice president of the Brooklyn Heights Association), the City was persuaded to adopt a special Class S zone along Furman Street, restricting any waterfront development there to a height of 50 feet—or 20 feet less than the heights of the Promenade. That zoning was approved by the Board of Estimate, June 25, 1953.

Ms. Yu has followed this part of the story also, and she brings it up to date. She notes that the Class S zone was abolished in 1961 as part of the city's comprehensive new zoning resolution, and that an abortive 1966 proposal by Vito P. Battista for a mile-long entertainment plaza parallel to the Promenade raised new fears that the "Promenade view could be up for grabs by sneaky developers."

In September 1974, Ms. Yu writes, the City Planning Commission granted a special scenic district designation to the Heights Promenade, the first to get such a designation, requiring that any threatening construction would first have to be approved by both the Planning Commission and the Board of Estimate.

Ms. Yu finds that the 1974 designation represented a significant advance over the 1953 one: "The earlier zoning designation was promulgated primarily to preserve property values of the fashionable Brooklyn Heights area where property values were enhanced by the Promenade's existence. The more recent designation seemed to have as its purpose a more sincere desire to preserve an outstanding scenic view."

The idea for her paper, Ms. Yu says, was suggested by her professor, Alexander Cooper, who, as a member of the city's Urban Design Group during the Lindsay years, had come to wonder about

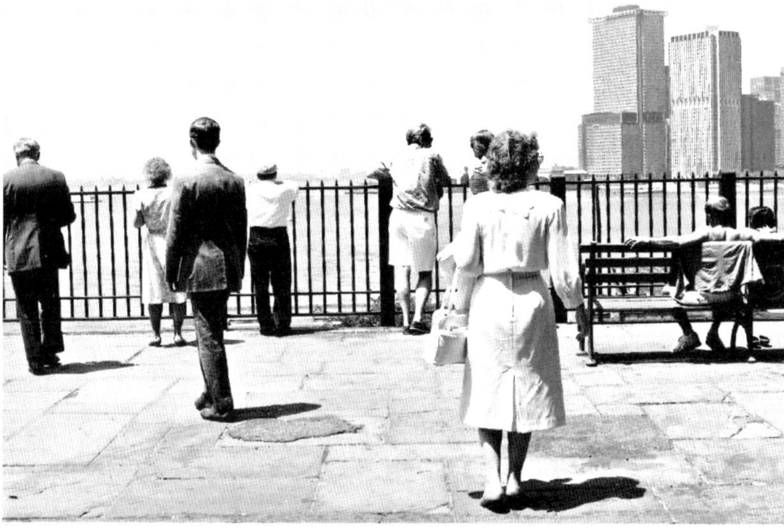

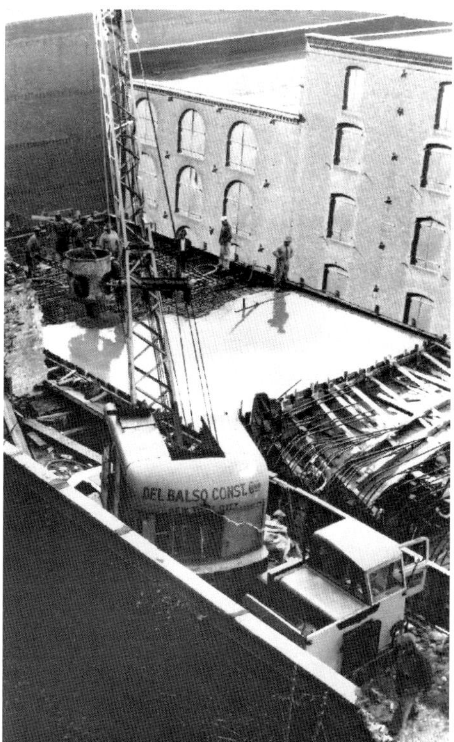

Above: People in all configurations may be seen on the Promenade. These, looking as stiff as statues, were spotted in July 1993.

Left: A Del Balso Company construction crane stands at the edge of the Heights as a worker is reflected in newly laid wet concrete of what appears to be the Promenade, perhaps early 1949. Note the warehouses on the west side of Furman Street. *Photo by Louise Casey.*

the origin of the Promenade. Her paper is titled: "The Brooklyn Heights Promenade: How Did It Happen?"

Which seems apt. Brooklyn has no Haussmann, no L'Enfant to work a boulevard or esplanade into a grand traffic scheme. No politician made the Promenade his baby. Even Robert Moses—though he put in the telling word when pressed—stood aside to let it take shape. All in all, the Promenade came about in a remarkably democratic and collaborative way.

For Brooklyn—and the world—how much better so. By contrast, look at the mess Cashmore and his friends made of Cadman Plaza and the Civic Center.

"Moses Writes Second Letter on Origins of Heights Promenade: More Material Comes to Light on Roles Played by Heights Residents"

Brooklyn Heights Press and Cobble Hill News, June 21, 1979

Robert Moses, former city construction coordinator, has written us a second letter about the Brooklyn Heights Promenade, and several persons have provided us with reminiscences or guided us to documents that should help establish how the decision to build the promenade was arrived at.

Mr. Moses says, "I know that I never heard of the Pierrepont Proposal until you wrote me." He is referring to a 19th-century proposal for a promenade by Heights landowner and developer Hezekiah Pierrepont.

Mr. Moses also writes, "I don't remember Mr. Nitardy, although I was friendly with Mrs. James, and my people were in more or less constant touch with people in the neighborhood."

The references there are to Columbia Heights properly owner Ferdinand W. Nitardy, credited by some with planting the germ of the promenade idea into Moses' head, and Mrs. Darwin James, whose husband helped Moses get his first (short-lived) New York City appointment in 1914, and who, herself, championed the preservation of the Heights in the period following World War II. Mr. Moses has denied that either of them influenced the decision to build the Promenade.

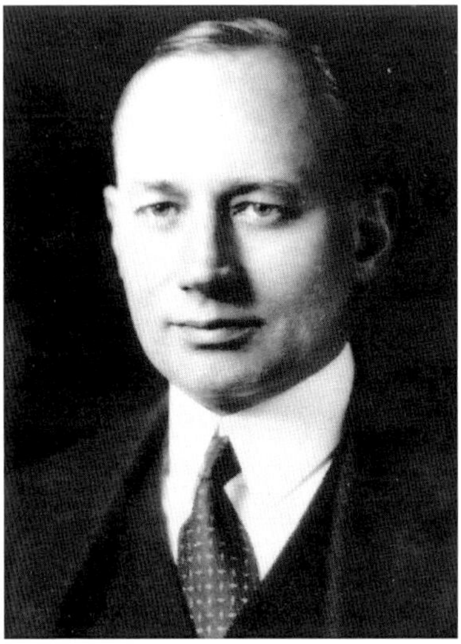

Paul Windels turned down an offer by Robert Moses to claim the original idea for the Promenade. Windels had been more interested in seeking public access to the waterfront. *Paul Windels Jr.*

Meanwhile, we have received indications of the roles played by Roy M.D. Richardson, who was president of the Brooklyn Heights Association at the time the final plans for the Furman Street section of the Brooklyn-Queens Expressway were being made, and by Paul Windels, who was not only a prominent Heights resident but had been the city's corporation counsel and had on various occasions served as a political mediator between Mayor Fiorello LaGuardia and the master builder, Robert Moses.

We expect shortly to examine the Roy Richardson papers on file at Brooklyn College. Another, possibly key, document has been furnished to us by Marina Yu, the Columbia graduate student whose previous research formed the basis for an article in these pages earlier this year ("The Promenade: Origins of a Miracle in Urban Design," BHP, Feb. 8, 1979). The document is the transcript of the March 10, 1943 City Planning Commission hearing, at which Messrs. Richardson, Nitardy and Windels spoke of the need for modifying the BQE's design, and Robert Moses raised the possibility of a promenade.

These documents, as well as the minutes of BHA governors' meetings furnished by BHA President George Silver, and the tips provided us by Mrs. Roy Richardson (with an assist from her daughter, Lois Burdick), Haughton Bell, Paul Windels Jr., Calvert Crary and Raymond C. Ingersoll (son of John Cashmore's predecessor as Brooklyn borough president), and Mrs. F.W. Nitardy, have given us fascinating glimpses into how the Promenade came to be built, and we are piecing the story together for a forthcoming issue. Here is the latest Robert Moses letter in full:

Dear Mr. Krogius:

I realize that the historical background of many of the public improvements made in the City of New York is of great interest, but without digging into the minutes of the City Planning Commission meetings held more than thirty-six years ago, it would be impossible to give you any accurate information on details of the events leading up to the construction of the promenade. I know that I never heard of the Pierrepont proposal until you wrote me. I don't remember Mr. Nitardy, although I was friendly with Mrs. James, and my people were in more or less constant touch with people in the neighborhood.

It would have been impractical and probably illegal to use public funds to build grass plots or front yards for those people fronting on the promenade. It certainly was in the public interest, as well as in the interest of the adjacent property owners, to build the promenade as a buffer against the traffic noises emanating from the expressway. It also provided one of the most magnificent views of the harbor and made it available for the general public. Although I have not personally seen it, I have been told that the view has been used by the moving picture and television industries and photographers.

It was a unique design for the highway and was certainly much more to the advantage of the community than attempting to blast through it from the vicinity of the Fort Greene Houses to connect with the Gowanus Parkway.

Cordially,
Robert Moses

Mr. Moses, now 90 years old, last wrote us on May 24 of this year, in reply to a request for his recollections as to how the promenade decision was reached. He regretted that he had no precise recollection, but denied that Mr. Nitardy or Mrs. James "influenced the decision to build the public promenade."

The new letter has come in response to the article that was subsequently published and forwarded to him. In the final paragraph Mr. Moses is evidently referring to a proposal for the BQE that would have avoided Brooklyn Heights altogether.

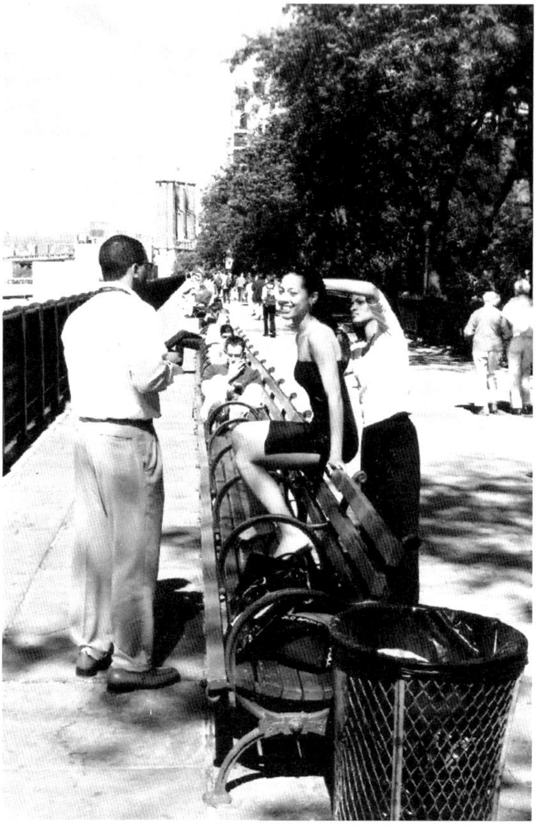

Left: A model has her hair adjusted for a photo shoot on the Promenade in September 2000. In 1979, at age ninety, Robert Moses wrote to the author, "Although I have not personally seen it, I have been told that the view has been used by the moving picture and television industries and photographers."

Below: Some of the photography seen on the Promenade is quite athletic. Here, a model leaps from a bench, with the Manhattan skyline setting at her back, in January 1986.

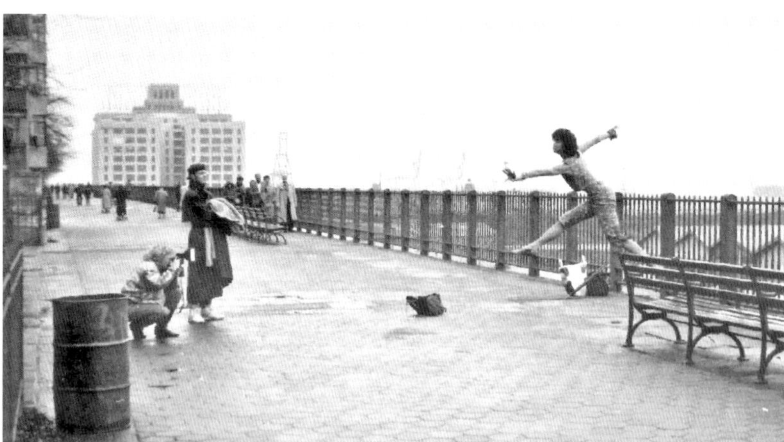

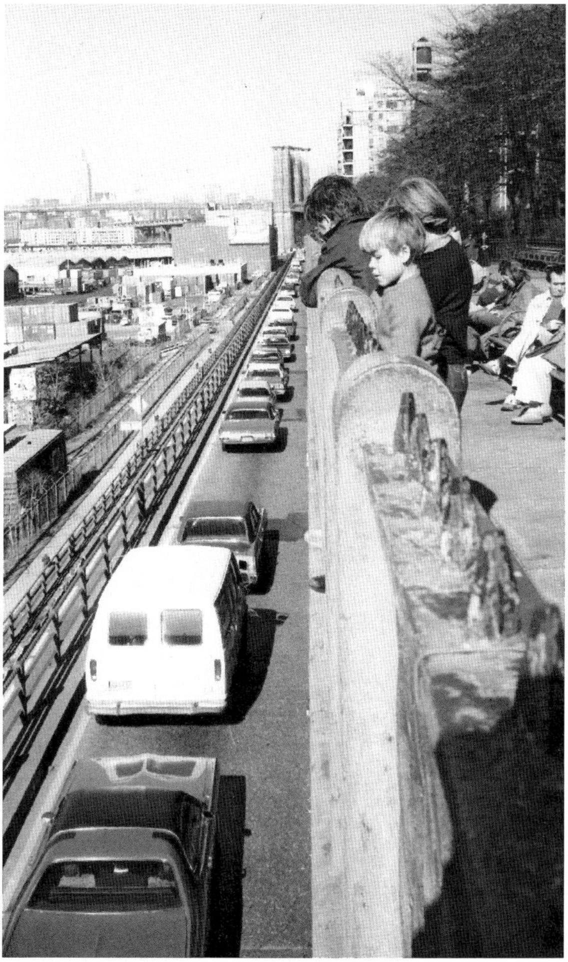

Boys peered over the Promenade's railing at traffic on the deck below on an October day in 1981.

In speaking of "grass plots or front yards" he is no doubt thinking of Mr. Nitardy's proposal, backed by the BHA, to place a "cover" on the BQE and restore the existing gardens on that cover.

And a final small note: Mr. Moses obviously does not mean that he has not personally seen the view from the Promenade—he was there at its opening, if not on other occasions—but that he has not seen movie or television crews at work there.

"Pre-Promenade: Did an Heiress Stop Heights 'Grand Concourse'? How a Heights Legend Grew Out of Fears BQE Would Cut the Neighborhood in Two"

Brooklyn Heights Press, December 10, 1981

Five days before Pearl Harbor, New York City Planning Commission Chairman Edwin A. Salmon spoke to the governors of the Brooklyn Heights Association about the plans for an express highway connecting Brooklyn and Queens.

"Among the possibilities under consideration," the minutes of that December 2, 1941, meeting noted, were "a covered highway along Furman Street, which would possibly have two or three levels, and an elevated highway along the waterfront."

That is the earliest hint I have found of the eventual Heights Promenade, which was to be formally completed on Pearl Harbor Day, December 7, ten years later.

Now, after thirty years of enjoying the completed Promenade, we still are not sure just how and where the idea for it originated, or who deserves the major credit for working out its design.

Fred Tuemmler of the City Planning Department drew up a proposal for the highway in 1939 as part of the city's then newly projected Master Plan and suggested two cantilevered roadway decks along a portion of the Heights; but Tuemmler, who died last month a few weeks before his eightieth birthday, did not propose the pedestrian deck on top.

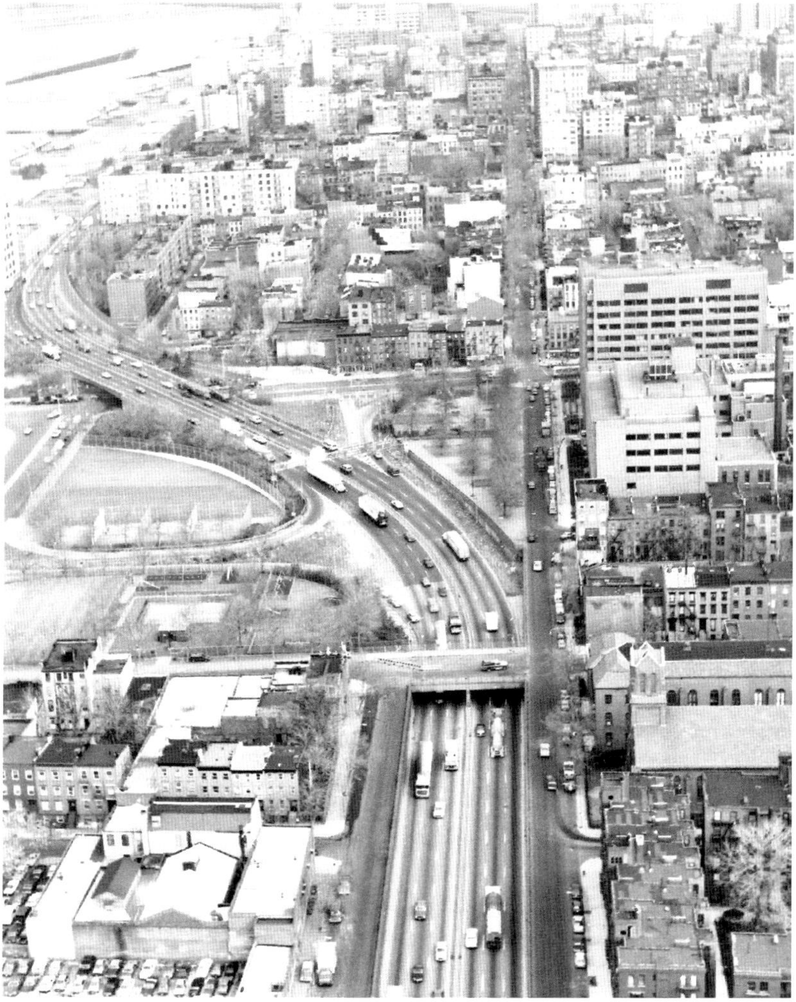

A 1987 aerial view by Andrea Pearl, then the Heights Press photographer, shows the BQE in the Hicks Street cut at lower center bending west across Atlantic Avenue to continue along Furman Street, skirting the edge of Brooklyn Heights. *From a* Brooklyn Heights Press *file.*

There is no indication that Commissioner Salmon was proposing a promenade either, or that his hearers took the idea of a "covered" highway to mean that the public should walk on the cover. Rather, they seem to have thought mainly in terms of a shield against traffic

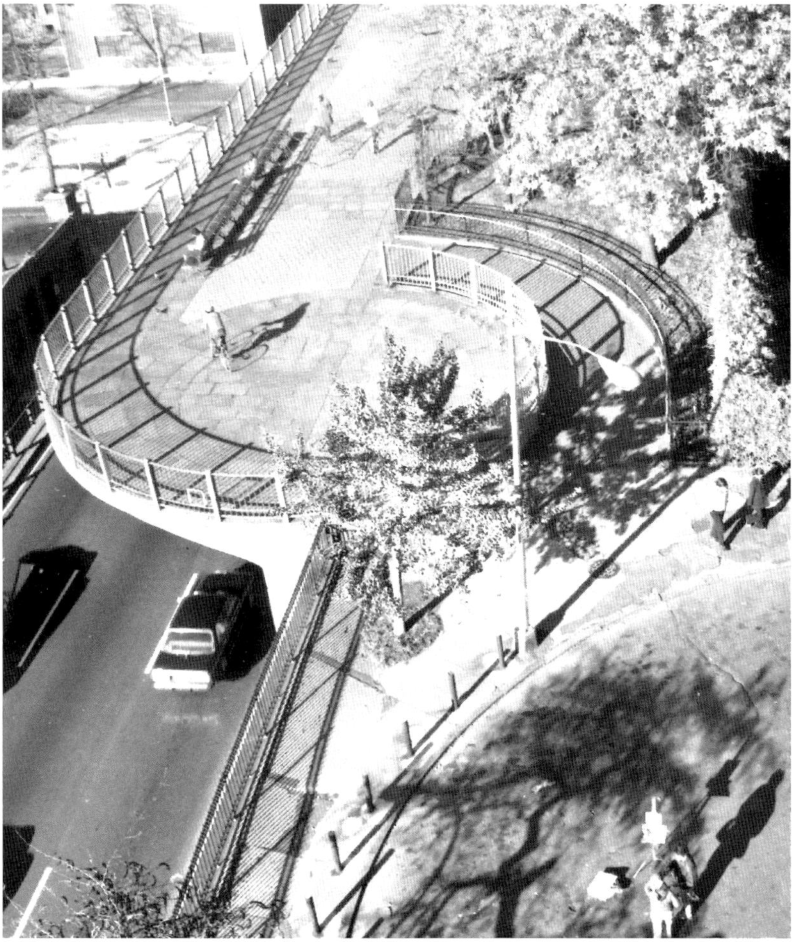

The southern circular end of the Promenade at Remsen Street, photographed in 1981, corresponds to the northern terminus. A member of a second firm, Clarke and Rapuano, which was contracted for the Promenade's landscaping, contended that the Andrews and Clark firm did not possess the design sensibility for this refined treatment. He maintained that Michael Rapuano was the designer but could not supply proof.

noise and fumes and perhaps of a deck on which the rear gardens of Columbia Heights brownstones could be re-established.

Nevertheless, the notion of "cover" was ultimately to be translated into a public expanse.

Before that could happen, however, there was to be an apparently serious setback to local hopes for a highway that the Heights neighborhood could live with.

Six alternate routes were being studied by the engineering firm of Andrews and Clark under contract to the Brooklyn borough president's office, ostensibly to relate the proposed highway to Borough President John Cashmore's dreams for a new civic center; but inasmuch as the firm was a favorite of Robert Moses', it was no doubt engaged at the park commissioner's behest.

The word got out that Moses favored a route that would cut the Heights in two, opening a 160-foot wide gash along Hicks Street and curving to join Tillary Street.

Ernest J. Clark, who at 76 remains active as senior partner of Andrews and Clark, recalled in a recent interview in his office that it was to be something "like the Grand Concourse in the Bronx."

Such an alarming prospect sent shivers through Brooklyn Heights. The city had, after all, approved the widening of Hicks Street on the other side of Atlantic Avenue, and that part of Hicks was to suffer a fate worse than getting a Grand Concourse.

There is widespread belief among many older Heights residents that Mrs. Darwin James III played a decisive role in making sure the highway would not bisect the Heights.

Gladys Underwood James was well known for her part in refurbishing the brownstone charm of the Heights and blocking high-rise apartment development after she and her husband bought the mansion-like brownstone at 2 Pierrepont Place in 1948; but in the fall of 1942—the time of the highway scare—she was living on an estate at Glen Head, Long Island. Born on Washington Avenue in the Bedford-Stuyvesant section, the typewriter heiress evidently always insisted that her move to the Heights was a "move back" to Brooklyn from farther out on the island.

At any rate, the story has it that when Mrs. James learned of the dreadful plan, she invited Robert Moses over to dinner and—armed with diagrams and maps—persuaded him that the route would be fatal to the neighborhood, and that the highway must be put along Furman Street.

Some persons who knew Mrs. James (she died in 1975) say she was joined in this effort by Mrs. Alice Campbell Good, who was the daughter of Rep. Felix Campbell and herself a Democratic National Committee-woman. Mrs. Good was to buy Number 3 Pierrepont Place, adjoining Number 2, in 1945; and she also did not live on the Heights in 1942. Yet a third person who has been mentioned as being present at the dinner of persuasion was Mary Carroll (Mrs. Otis Swan Carroll), who did live in the Heights in 1942.

There is no doubt that Mrs. James knew Robert Moses well. Several persons have attested that they personally met him at Mrs. James' in subsequent years. Mrs. James' father-in-law, the banker Darwin James II, had been a member of the three-man civil service commission under Mayor John Purroy Mitchel to whose staff the young Bob Moses was appointed in 1914, and for which he wrote some highly praised, but never enacted, recommendations for civil service reform.

Mrs. Anna O'Sullivan, who was a housekeeper for the Jameses for many years, was reached in Miami recently, thanks to the help of one of Mrs. James' daughters, Mrs. Nadine Coash. Mrs. O'Sullivan said she had heard Mrs. James refer to the dinner in question, but that she was not present at the time and did not know where it might have been held. She recalled that the Jameses had belonged to the Heights Casino since well before World War II, and that Mrs. James had an interest in Heights affairs before she moved here.

Another concerned resident, who says he "rushed there to Moses" when he heard of the threat, is B. Meredith Langstaff, author of *Brooklyn Heights: Yesterday—Today—Tomorrow* (Brooklyn Heights Association, 1937) and president of the Brooklyn Heights Association in the late nineteen-forties.

Langstaff told me he "suggested the plan that is there now of having two things hanging out from the Heights," meaning the cantilevered roadways, running "one way this way and the other that way, and not have a lot of noise to bother people on the Heights." However, he said he did not suggest a promenade on top.

We do have documentation that Roy M.D. Richardson, then president of the Brooklyn Heights Association, wrote to Planning

Commission Chairman Salmon on September 15, 1942, expressing concern about "a rumor current on the Heights" that a boulevard might be run through the area. We have Salmon's not entirely reassuring reply that "all suggestions for replanning, rezoning, arterial improvements and other civic developments" would be placed before civic organizations and the public "before any part of the plan is finally adopted."

We also have a letter from Mrs. Genevieve B. Earle, the City Council Minority Leader and a resident of 11 Cranberry Street, who was herself interested in keeping the Heights attractive. In an October 5, 1942, reply to Richardson noting that the feared route was "one of several proposed for this highway," she said she could notify him about "the proposed plans when they have reached a more definite stage."

(I am particularly grateful to Mrs. Roy M.D. Richardson for directing me to her late husband's files at the Brooklyn College library, for they contain some of the best evidence I have come across as to the developments that led to the creation of the Promenade.)

Large as it looms in Heights legend, the story of the confrontation with Moses over the Heights-bisecting route is one I confess I have been skeptical of. Was it really the route Moses wanted? Why would he have preferred it over the Furman Street route?

"All except the one around Furman Street," Ernest Clark remarked of the various alternatives, "couldn't meet expressway standards, like curves, and would cut through very expensive property and churches. Then it boiled down that the route around Furman Street would be the most logical way to go."

Recently, however, I got some corroboration of the Moses devil theory from former City Planning Commission member Lawrence M. Orton, who said Moses "wanted the route to be turned right toward the heart of Brooklyn. We thought it was a foolish idea."

Orton felt Moses opposed the Furman Street route because it had come out of the City Planning Commission's offices before he was a member of the commission (he became one in 1942) and because he didn't want to be bound by the Master Plan.

(In Robert A. Caro's biography, *The Power Broker: Robert Moses and the Fall of New York*, Knopf, 1947, Orton emerges as something of a hero who tried, often in vain, to bring a concern for people and neighborhoods into the working out of Moses' highway and housing projects.)

Two and a half years ago, in gathering information for an earlier article on the Promenade's origins ("That is Not a Promenade…," *Brooklyn Heights Press*, July 12, 1979), I talked to Paul Windels Jr., who recalled his father telling him that "Moses had wanted to tear up the pedestrian walk on the Brooklyn Bridge" (Moses liked to build his bridges, like the Verrazano, without pedestrian walks), and was angered when the Brooklyn Heights Association helped block that plan, and felt vindictive toward the Heights.

The elder Windels, as Robert Caro notes, served as a go-between for those two egotistical figures, Robert Moses and Fiorello LaGuardia, and knew Moses well.

There is a reference to the Brooklyn Bridge walkway in Roy Richardson's May 14, 1943, annual report to his membership: "The Association last year was instrumental in keeping the footwalk on Brooklyn Bridge open to pedestrians during certain hours," though he added that the organization was now complying with the Navy's decision to close the walk for the duration of the war.

So there may have been a real, if brief, confrontation between the wishes of Moses and the wishes of the neighborhood over the route the expressway was to take. Certainly the memories of one are strong even if the details are scant.

By early the following year the route was, in any event, once more mapped along Furman Street, but an unquestioned confrontation was at hand over the form it was to take.

A footnote to the Gladys James story: One version of the legend has it that, as part of a deal to secure the Promenade, Mrs. James offered to give the property occupied by the Henry E. Pierrepont mansion at 1 Pierrepont Place to the city for a playground. From a letter by Roy Richardson, dated January 8, 1942, it becomes clear that the city was already then taking steps to buy the Pierrepont property for a park, and the governors of the Heights Association had unanimously approved the city purchase (the mansion was demolished in 1946)—all this with no reference to Mrs. James, and well before she bought 2 Pierrepont Place. Also, no connection seems

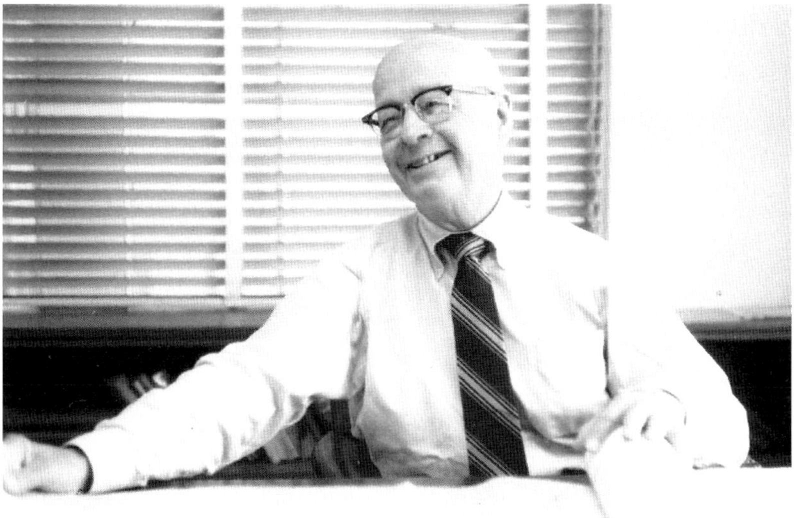

Ernest J. Clark (the project engineer for the BQE's construction), seen here in 1981, said that the design of the Promenade evolved through a collaborative team effort involving the study of many possible ways to construct the Furman Street section. He dismissed claims of any individual's unique inspiration for the solution that came to be adopted.

to have been implied between the acquisitions of the Pierrepont playground and the BQE. After all, the final route of the BQE had not yet been settled on, much less any talk of a promenade!

"What's in a Name? 'Esplanade' Fancier Finds Vulgarity in 'Promenade'"

Brooklyn Heights Press, December 10, 1981

The Promenade Restaurant referred to in this article was a diner on Montague Street at Hicks, a corner since occupied by the Heights Café. The typewriter heiress Gladys Underwood James anticipated the landmark preservation movement by strategically buying Brooklyn Heights brownstones to forestall apartment developments.

You can get an argument over who deserves the major credit for the creation of the pedestrian deck above the BQE at Furman Street.

You can also get an argument over what that deck should be called: Esplanade or Promenade?

Gladys James, who is discussed in the accompanying article on the routing of the BQE, was a champion of "esplanade."

There are early references, both before and during its construction, to both names. The little booklet given out by the Borough President's office for the official ceremony marking the pedestrian deck's completion thirty years ago—December 7, 1951—called it the "Columbia Heights Promenade."

The AIA Guide to New York City distinguishes between the ostensibly formal "esplanade" and the popular "promenade."

Mrs. Tracy S. Voorhees, who was a friend of Mrs. James, says

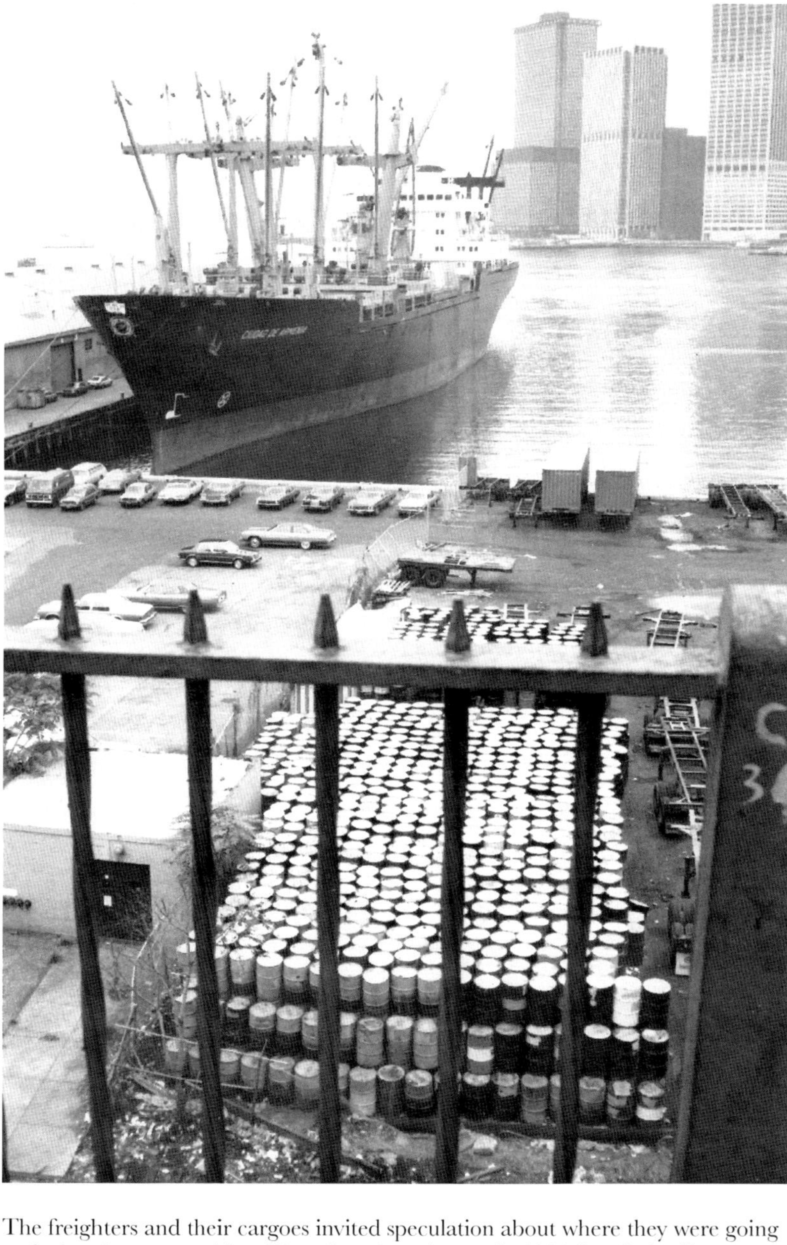

The freighters and their cargoes invited speculation about where they were going and what they were taking. Were those barrels seen in 1981 for oil, fertilizer or something else?

of the latter term, "Gladys James and I fought for a while, but I gave it up." She explains: "The Promenade restaurant spoiled it for that [Esplanade]."

J. Victor Herd argues that "esplanade" is the more correct "inasmuch as it looks out over the water." Indeed, several dictionaries I have checked associate a water view with an esplanade but not necessarily with a promenade, though there is the compound term "promenade deck" (of a ship) which has a certain appropriateness in describing the appearance of the walk above the BQE.

Mrs. Voorhees, also making the point about a water view, finds in addition a negative connotation to "promenade" as implying a certain vulgar showiness: "Promenade always seemed like Peacock Alley at the old Waldorf where people liked to show off their clothes."

In next week's article discussing the hearing that produced the perhaps crucial exchanges between Robert Moses and Heights representative Roy Richardson, F.W. Nitardy, and Paul Windels, we'll come to Moses' remark: "That is not a promenade." Moses was not talking about definitions or semantics. He was discussing public access to the view from the Heights, and it just may be that the solution of having a pedestrian deck as cover for the BQE became a real likelihood at that moment.

If so, the term "promenade" can be said to have been there at the birth. The term "esplanade" also came into play at that hearing several minutes later.

"BQE Planner, Born in Brooklyn, Gained Note in Capital Region"

Brooklyn Heights Press, January 14, 1982

The man who, in his own words, "was responsible for the conceptual design for the cantilevered section" of the Brooklyn-Queens Expressway was a Brooklyn native and attended Manhattan Training (now John Jay) High School.

Fred W. Tuemmler, whose preliminary studies for the BQE were discussed here last month ("Heights Promenade at Age 30: New Light Shed on its Origins," BHP, Dec. 3, 1981) was a largely self-made professional, according to a letter and biographical sketch received from his son, Dr. William B. Tuemmler of Laguna Niguel, California.

Born Frederick William Tuemmler, the future planner of highways, downtowns, shopping centers, and parks lived as a child and young man on Himrod Street, which traverses the Bushwick and Ridgewood sections of Brooklyn.

"He was a self-made professional man in that he did not receive a college degree," Dr. Tuemmler writes, "although he took a number of courses and did obtain a certificate in urban planning [from the State University of New York]. He was thus largely self-educated and, I must say, admirably so."

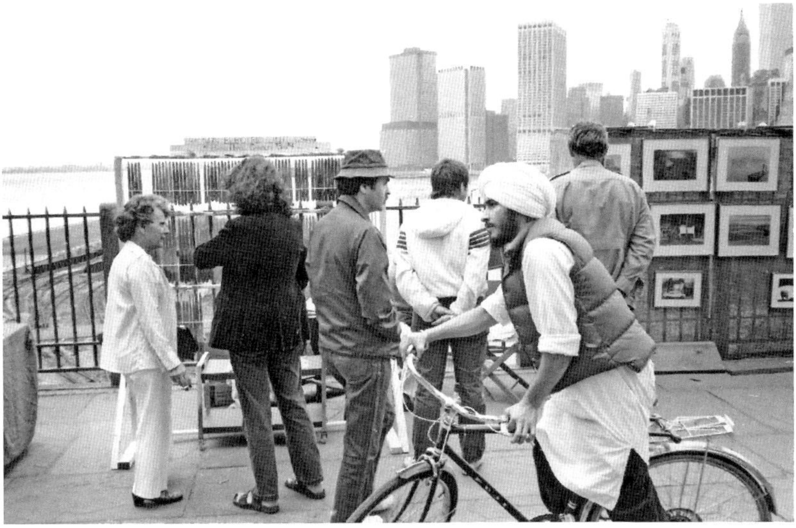

Semiannual art shows on the Promenade in the 1970s and '80s drew even more than the usual numbers and kinds of visitors, as here in May 1982. (The prohibition against bicycle riding has been much disregarded through the years.) The art shows were finally discontinued after they had started attracting too many vendors of trinkets and kitsch.

Dr. Tuemmler notes that his father became president of the Washington chapter of the American Institute of Planners, as well as being on the board of governors of the national organization, and was an honorary life member of the American Society of Planning Officials.

Fred Tuemmler died November 2, 1981, in Hagerstown, Md., a few weeks before his eightieth birthday.

Although he served in the topographic and public works offices of the Queens Borough President from 1925 to 1939 and with the City Planning Department from 1939 until November 1941, he gained prominence in the Maryland-Virginia-Washington, D.C. area. He became Director of Planning for the Maryland National Capital Park and Planning Commission in 1941 and went into private practice as a planning consultant in 1953.

Having been principal author of "A Proposal for a Brooklyn-Queens East River Express Highway," City Planning Department,

January 30, 1940—a proposal that included partly canilevered roadways as part of a "special treatment" of the highway along Furman Street—Tuemmler was thus absent from the New York scene during the crucial months of 1942–43 when the Furman Street route was finally agreed upon and the three-deck cantilevered—including the Promenade—was adopted as the design.

Tuemmler's proposal would have run the BQE's southern section at grade level along Columbia Street instead of in its present deep cut along Hicks Street, would have carried it around Fulton Ferry north of the Heights, and in general would have sought to minimize the expressway's impact on residential neighborhoods—a concern not greatly shared by Robert Moses, the man who eventually got the BQE built.

Of his father's proposal, Dr. Tuemmler writes: "I cannot help but reflect that his efforts on the BQE were more than a little inspired by his desire to do something special for his beloved Brooklyn."

Dr. Tuemmler, who is vice president of research and development for the Hooker Chemical Company, can only speculate as to whether his father, as "an imaginative and creative man," entertained any thought of a promenade, adding, "However, in the austere days of 1939, if one was asked to design an expressway, that is probably what one did."

As to the yet unresolved question of whether Fred Tuemmler's proposal in fact influenced the final design, former Planning Commission Vice Chairman Lawrence M. Orton makes this point: "I have long felt that a reasonably gifted professional who can commit his ideas to understandable form carries a lot more weight and has more influence than is often accorded."

In other words, good paperwork can be more important than politics in carrying the day.

If so, Fred Tuemmler certainly presented any successor who cared to study it with a clear analysis of the problem and a well-reasoned potential solution.

He himself evidently thought he had influenced the outcome.

At the age of 77, standing six feet, weighing 140 pounds, Fred Tuemmler applied for a part-time job as Planning Administrator of the City of Hagerstown and submitted a ten-page biographical sketch.

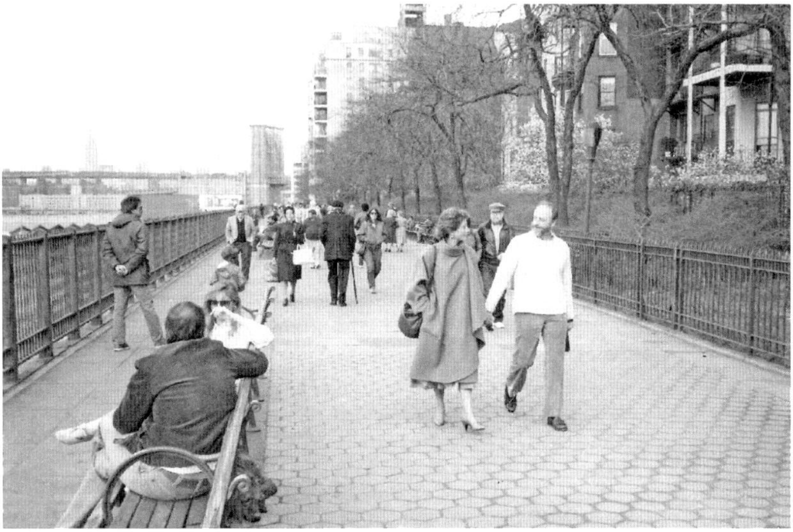

The coming of spring, here in April 1985, has always encouraged romantic visits to the Promenade.

In it Tuemmler described himself in the third person and said this of his BQE role: "He was responsible for the conceptual design for the cantilevered section of the Brooklyn shorefront highway which was part of the then-proposed Brooklyn-Queens Expressway. The shorefront section has since then been completed substantially in accordance with Mr. Tuemmler's concept."

"The Promenade: Was It Moses' Revenge Against the Heights?"

Brooklyn Heights Press, March 4, 1982

Attempts to unlock the secret of how Brooklyn Heights happened to get its Promenade keep being redirected to the enigmatic personality of Robert Moses.

A controversial clue dropped last weekend by John G. Hunter has prompted a new look at the story of a great Moses project that was frustrated: the Brooklyn-Battery Bridge.

Mr. Hunter recalled a 1960s dinner to which Brooklyn Heights Association officers had invited Mr. Moses. It was supposed to have been a friendly affair with local community leaders praising the Master Builder for the Promenade and other achievements and the great man graciously accepting the tribute.

Instead, Mr. Hunter recalled, the park commissioner launched into a diatribe over the blocking—back in 1939—of his proposed bridge. He vented his anger at the Heights resident who had persuaded the First Lady, Mrs. Eleanor Roosevelt, to oppose the bridge in her newspaper column, "My Day."

Since, on any reasonable ground, it is difficult to account for Robert Moses' disregard of the 1939–40 City Planning Department proposal to route a Brooklyn-Queens express highway along the edge of the Heights at Furman Street and his preference instead for a plan to cut through the heart of the Heights, one finds it hard to escape the conclusion that the desire to punish the Heights was an element of the commissioner's motivation.

When even his own engineers finally concluded that Furman Street was the best route, there is a rather persuasive suggestion that Mr. Moses then adopted the idea of a public promenade atop a double-deck highway partly in revenge against prominent Heights residents who would have preferred the re-instatement of private gardens above the highway.

Robert Moses was a different person to different people: loyal, affectionate, generous, charming, sentimental to those who worked with him or saw things his way; arrogant, ruthless, vindictive to those who disagreed with him or opposed him.

Evidence of Commissioner Moses' deep feelings on the subject of the Brooklyn-Battery crossing can be found in his own book, *Public Works: A Dangerous Trade* (McGraw-Hill, 1970). Having "fondly thought" he had disposed of the plan for a tunnel as against a bridge, Mr. Moses writes: "Suddenly, on Wednesday, April 5, 1939, Mrs. Eleanor Roosevelt, in her 'My Day' column in the *New York World Telegram*, leaped into the fray with her usual impetuosity. She wrote, apparently at the instance of personal friends living on Brooklyn Heights, as follows…"

He then reprints an excerpt from the column, including these words: "I have a plea from a man who is deeply interested in Manhattan Island, particularly in the beauty of the approach from the ocean at Battery Park. He tells me that a New York official, who is without doubt always efficient, is proposing a bridge one hundred feet high at the river, which will go across to the Whitehall Building over Battery Park. This, he says, will mean a screen of elevated roadways, pillars, etc., at that particular point. I haven't a question that this will be done in the name of progress, and something undoubtedly needs to be done. But isn't there room for some consideration of the preservation of the few beautiful spots that still remain to us on an over-crowded island?"

Remarking that "My Day" contained "an endless succession of noble impulses unsupported by thought or evidence," Commissioner Moses characterizes the daily column as "the product of confused early education, a cloistered girlhood, and sudden precipitation into world affairs."

President Franklin D. Roosevelt himself came into the fray. After several months of maneuverings, which included Secretary of War Harry H. Woodring's caution that the bridge would be "seaward of a vital naval establishment [the Brooklyn Navy Yard]," the President wrote to the commissioner on October 30, 1939, that "the construction of the bridge would not be in the best interests of national defense."

It had taken the President of the United States to stop Robert Moses, and the line of communication that led to him had been opened from Brooklyn Heights.

Mr. Moses, in his book, finds it "interesting to note" that Secretary Woodring resigned shortly after his intervention in the matter, and he adds: "The shallowness of the Secretary's reasoning

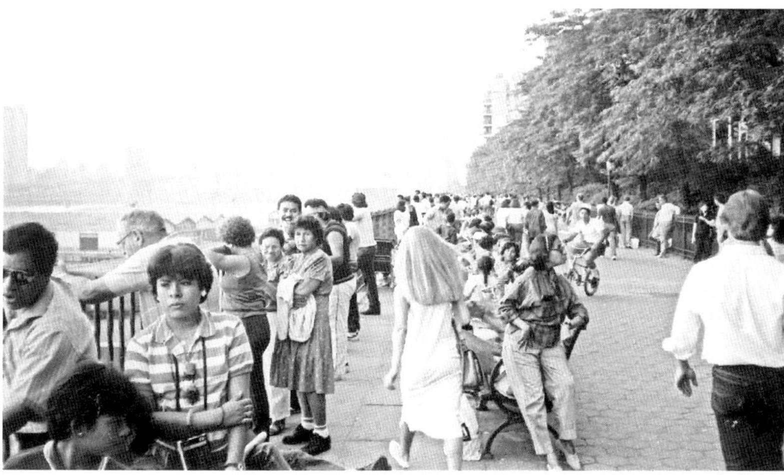

The Promenade's popularity as a holiday gathering place is evident from this photo taken on July 4, 1985. Crowds would come early to get good places for viewing the fireworks held in the East River on the Fourth and other special occasions, like the 1983 centennial of the opening of the Brooklyn Bridge. Police have often had to limit the number of people allowed onto the Promenade at such times. In 2010 and 2011 the Fourth of July fireworks were held on the Hudson River, behind the Manhattan skyscrapers—to protests from Brooklyn. Often, though, and without advance notice, private fireworks displays are held on the East River, to the enjoyment of the lucky ones who happen to be on the Promenade at the right time.

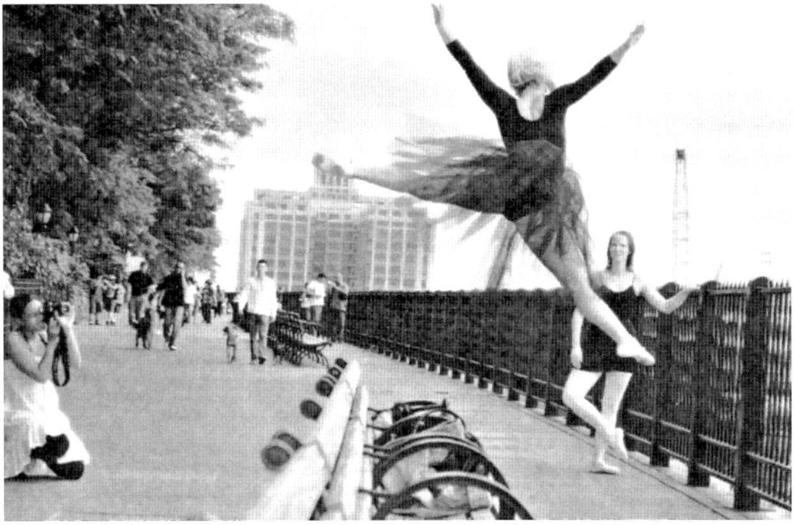

An exuberant ballet student soars above a Promenade bench in June 2009, while a fellow dancer watches and another takes a photograph.

and its dubious motivation became obvious in the light of the subsequent approval of the Verrazano-Narrows Bridge 'seaward of the Navy Yard.'"

"Triborough took its licking and went to work on a tunnel," Mr. Moses then writes, depersonalizing his hurt into a defeat suffered by the impersonal Triborough Bridge and Tunnel Authority that he headed. He concludes this section of his book with "One final comment—I crawled into Bartlett's *Quotations* in 1950 with this gem: 'A tunnel is merely a tiled, vehicular bathroom smelling faintly of monoxide.' My slightly poisonous words did not, however, survive this edition and I am no longer among Bartlett's immortals."

Who was the Heights resident (or residents) who got the ear of Mrs. Roosevelt? Mr. Hunter's impression is that Commissioner Moses referred to a woman in his remarks at that unfortunate dinner.

For her part, Mrs. Roosevelt wrote in her column of "a man who is deeply interested in Manhattan Island..."

Robert A. Caro, in *The Power Broker: Robert Moses and the Fall of New York* (Knopf, 1974), says that the city's reform leaders, unhappy about the prospect of a Brooklyn-Battery bridge, asked former City Corporation Counsel Paul Windels—a Heights resident who lived on Pineapple Street—to confer with the veteran reformer and lawyer, Charles C. Burlingham. According to Mr. Caro, Mr. Burlingham told Mr. Windels: “Call Eleanor.”

"A Few Statistics"

Brooklyn Heights Press, December 6, 2001

The Promenade is 1,850 feet long, a bit over a third of a mile. Situated on a deck cantilevered from the escarpment of Brooklyn Heights, it is part of a reinforced concrete structure that includes two traffic decks below it. The walkway deck is 25 feet wide along most of its length, 32 feet where bays were made for rows of benches along its inland fence, and it has a clear pedestrian passage 16 feet wide for the strollers and joggers who move along its length.

The height of the Promenade above Furman Street varies between 50 and 53 feet. The two traffic decks are each 33.5 feet wide, with not quite 17 feet of each deck cantilevered. The bottom deck projects 15.5 feet across Furman Street. The entire reinforced-concrete structure extends inland about 42 feet from the eastern wall of Furman Street, for a total width of about 57 feet. Traffic on the upper deck is northbound, southbound on the lower.

A green strip 20 feet wide at most points, on the inland side of the Promenade, is planted with honey locust trees, shrubs and flowering plants. The 160 Columbia Heights apartment building is the only building that abuts directly on the walkway. On the base of the flagpole at the Montague Street entrance is a tablet commemorating Genevieve Beavers Earle, City Council Minority Leader, who

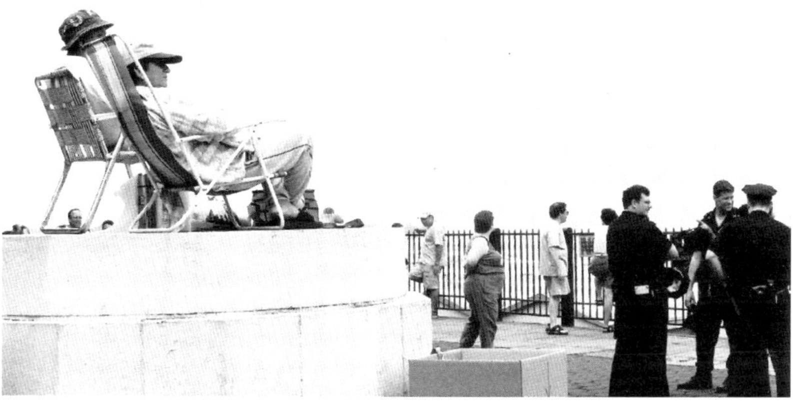

Two men found a comfortable vantage point in anticipation of viewing fireworks on July 4, 2000. The pedestal at the base of the Promenade's Orange Street entrance has otherwise remained empty, although in the 1980s, two competitions were held for a sculpture to commemorate the Roeblings, who envisioned and built the Brooklyn Bridge. A maquette by the South American artist Marisol, of a chariot with Emily Roebling holding a rooster of triumph, her husband Washington and father-in-law John behind her, was chosen. However, the Brooklyn Heights Association, which had sponsored the competitions, was unable to raise the funding to get the sculpture executed.

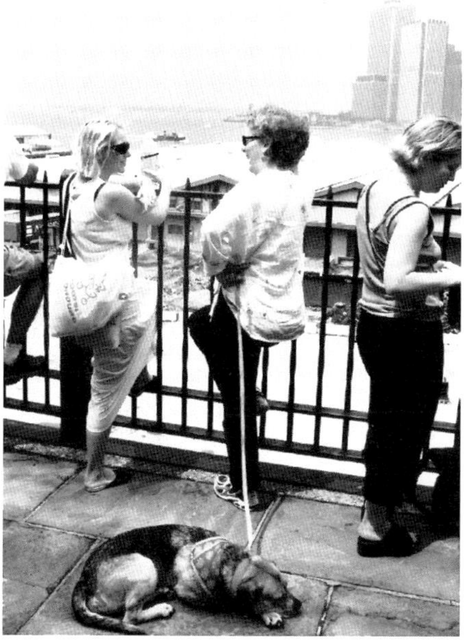

Neighborly conversations among the locals (who often also jog there) are as much a part of the Promenade as visits by tourists. This scene was captured in July 2000.

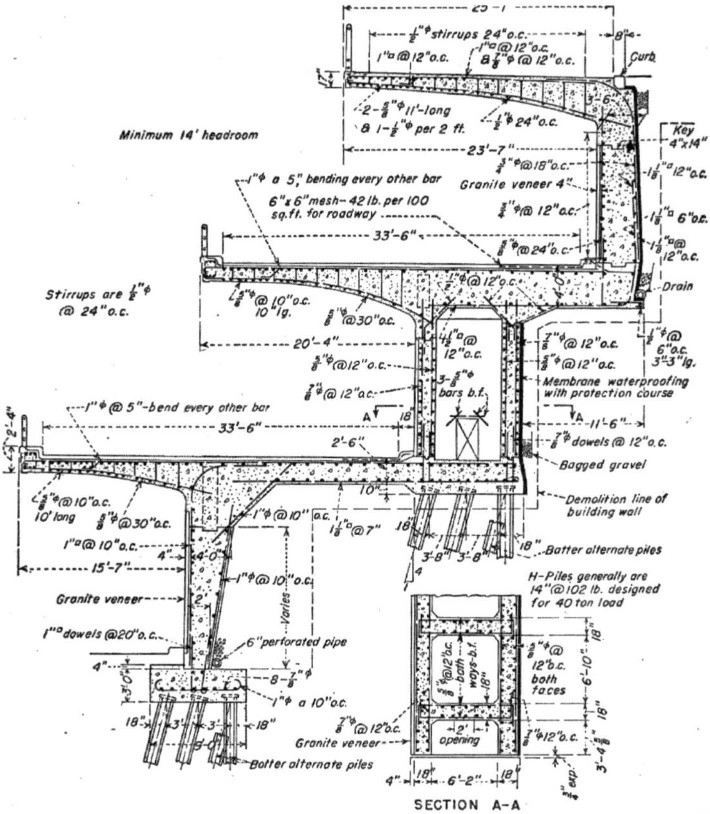

An engineering drawing detailing the specifications for a section of the BQE triple cantilever. The Promenade extends partway above the two traffic levels, the upper northbound and the lower southbound. Engineer Phillips H. Lovering of Andrews and Clark was credited with working out the precise form of the cantilever structure. A consulting engineer named Shortridge Hardesty advised extra stiffening, advice that was followed.

supported efforts to have the highway run along Furman Street and advocated attractive public access to the view from the Heights.

According to a 1948 article in *Engineering News-Record* by Phillips H. Lovering, designer of the cantilevers, the three-deck Promenade-BQE section was being built by the Del Balso Construction Corporation under a $5,836,000 contract.

"Forgot My Glasses"

Brooklyn Heights Press, December 6, 2001

Andrews & Clark engineer Phillips H. Lovering recalled in a letter a surprising fact about the head of Del Balso Construction, the company that built the cantilevered Promenade section.

"Our resident engineer frequently went to lunch with Mr. Del Balso who always said he had left his glasses in the office and asked what was on the menu," Lovering wrote. "Our resident engineer told us it took him a considerable time to discover that Mr. Del Balso was illiterate."

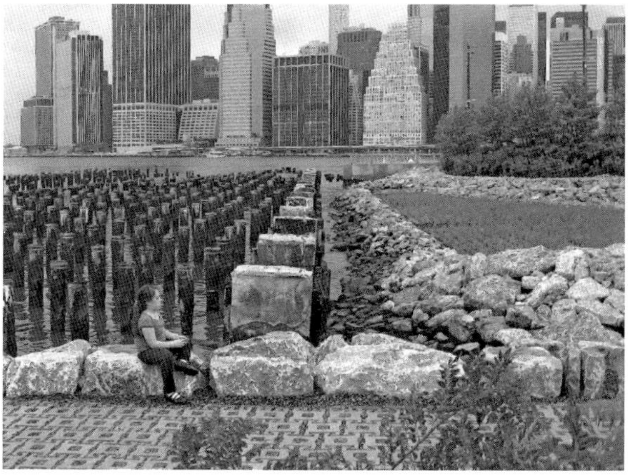

As a reminder of the historic waterfront below the Promenade, pilings that supported part of Pier 1 have been left in place. A small girl sat beside them in August 2010. *Photo by Mary Frost,* Brooklyn Eagle.

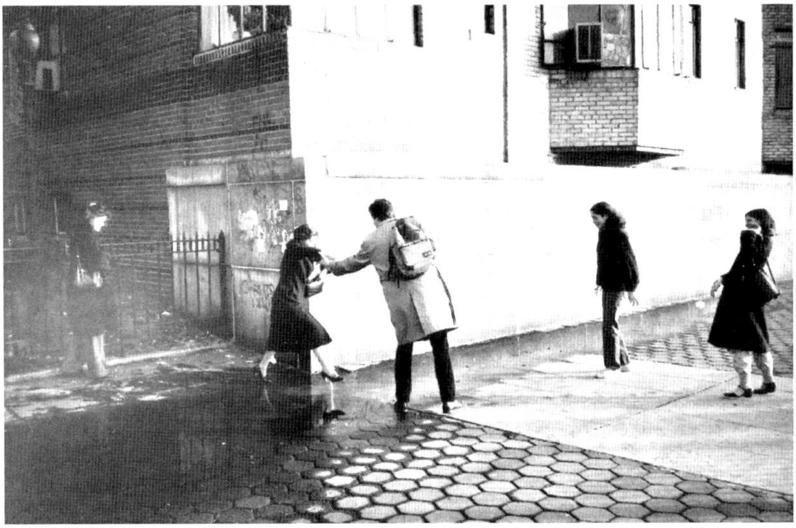

Above: The Promenade has undergone its share of wear and tear through the years, and rain has sometimes led to puddles at the junction of the concrete cantilever structure and the land behind it, as here in February 1983 at the Clark Street entrance, where the apartment building of 160 Columbia Heights is the only building to abut the Promenade directly. In the 1990s, another puddle, at the Pierrepont Street entrance, became so persistent that people took to calling it Lake Promenade. Subsequent repairs at entrance points along the Promenade's inner edge largely eliminated the problem.

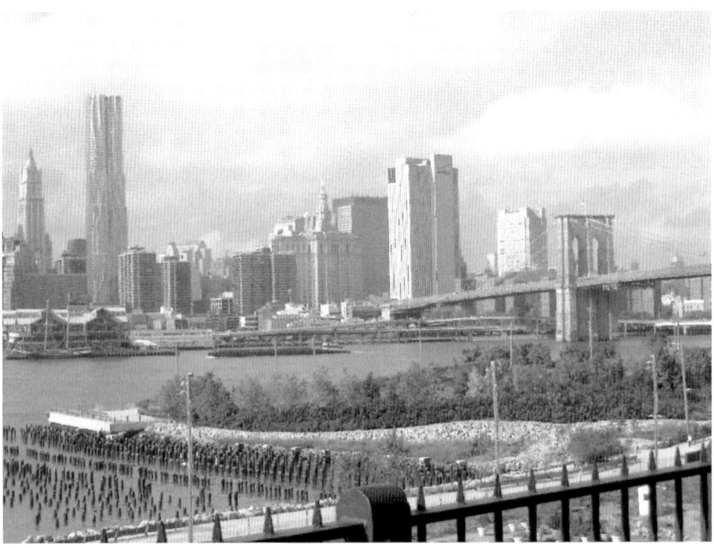

Still, Lovering thought Del Balso "deserves much credit for having started with one truck and sidewalk contracts and gradually enlarging his force until he was able to construct a project this size."

Left: With the freighters long gone, the long-held dream of a Brooklyn Bridge Park began to be realized, providing a new foreground to views from the Promenade. Where Pier 1 had been, new green had sprouted, as seen here in October 2011.

Appendix

Correspondence of Henrik Krogius

Letter from City Construction Coordinator Robert Moses to Henrik Krogius, dated May 11, 1953. The Board of Esimate to which Moses refers was later ruled to be in violation of the constitutional "one person, one vote" requirement and was abolished, and its powers devolved on the more representational city council.

Dear Lieutenant,

I have your letter of May 8. Frankly I don't think you have sufficiently studied the problem of zoning on the Heights and the protection of the Esplanade enough to understand it completely, otherwise I do not see how you could possibly figure out that we would fail to do everything legitimate to protect what we have created.

Without attempting to claim undue credit I think you will find that as a matter of historic fact I was one of those who originally suggested the Esplanade on the three story expressway system. It was adopted in the face of enormous opposition, including that of quite a few of the property owners who didn't want their back yards taken and bitterly opposed having the common run of folks use the walk.

From the very beginning, I have urged the protection of the view. We have more or less adequate protection from billboards within 200 feet under an amendment to the Zoning Resolution protecting parkways and expressways which was put through some years ago. Beyond this limit there is a question what will happen. It is claimed that an old forty-foot deed restriction dating back to the establishment of the docks and running with the land will stand up in the courts. Unfortunately this only covers a small part of the Esplanade and view. It should be noted that if this old deed restriction is supported by the courts, the zoning protection which we propose will have no adverse effect so far as this section is concerned. There is, however, considerable doubt about this, and whether or not the restriction would effectively screen out billboards. I would still prefer as a solution the condemnation of an aerial easement to protect the entire view from the Esplanade. We canvassed this idea pretty thoroughly when the rights of way for the expressway and esplanade were acquired originally, but no one knows what the awards would be and it would be impossible to get votes in the governing bodies of the city when there is no assurance as to cost.

If this condemnation device is eliminated because support cannot be obtained for it, we must fall back on restrictions in the zoning ordinance itself. The City cannot do a piece of spot zoning simply protecting this particular view. Therefore it is necessary to establish a new zone covering waterfront areas of this type. The City Planning Commission actually adopted a fifty foot zone of this type and it was approved by the Board of Estimate. The next step was to present a map establishing such zones at Brooklyn Heights and two other locations.

At this stage the City Planning Commission was put on notice by the Port of New York Authority, the Commissioner of Marine and Aviation, New York Dock Company and others that they were opposed to the adoption of the fifty foot zone on the Heights. All but the New York Dock Company were, however, willing to approve a seventy-foot restriction within 100 feet of the waterfront and 50 feet inshore from this line. The City Planning Commission then adopted a new zone with these restrictions, that is a seventy feet height restriction one hundred feet inshore of the bulkhead line and a fifty feet height restriction from that line to Furman Street.

The amended resolution establishing this zone is now before the Board of Estimate. Under the City Charter it becomes law if the Board does not act within thirty days. The Board may change the resolution but only by a three-fourths vote. If this new zone is adopted with or without amendments the individual maps fixing the district must thereafter be approved by the City Planning Commission and the Board of Estimate in the same manner.

The President of the Borough of Brooklyn may, if he wishes, move the rejection of the pending amendment in which case the former fifty-foot amendment will remain in force subject to the adoption of the individual maps. There is no evidence that if the Board of Estimate rejects the present amendment it will adopt a map under the original fifty-foot amendment. You must have in mind also that under the Charter when there is a protest by 20% of the area affected by the maps, it can only be adopted by unanimous vote of the Board of Estimate. They may reject both, in which case we would be nowhere. In the meantime several of us, led by Borough President Cashmore, are meeting with the Port of New York Authority again tomorrow to discuss the opposition of that agency and the Department of Marine and Aviation.

All of the above should serve to indicate to you how complex municipal government it, and what a mistake it is to criticize public officials without having a full understanding of their problems.

Cordially,
Robert Moses

Letter from City Construction Coordinator Robert Moses to Henrik Krogius, dated May 18, 1953.

Dear Lieutenant,

I have your letter of May 15. If the City Planning Commission now submits the Heights protection map under the existing fifty-foot amendment to the Zoning Resolution, there will no doubt be an opportunity to discuss the matter in the Board of Estimate. I don't think there will be any difficulty in the City Planning Commission. Those who support the present fifty-foot law should, of course, favor the adoption of the map. I have very little confidence in any new amendment incorporating the curious suggestions made by my friend Austin Tobin. I do not see for the life of me how any such suggestions could be adopted governing a new "S" District to be applied in several places besides the Heights.

The notion that the height below seventy-feet at the waterfront would be measured from the eyes of a person on a [*sic*] Esplanade is just too silly for words. There are places in the city where the district would apply, where there is no esplanade at all in the ordinary sense or esplanades of all sorts of heights.

I continue to be for definite action and not for gestures.

Cordially,
Robert Moses
Co-Ordinator

Letter from Henrik Krogius to Robert Moses, dated May 31, 1979.

Dear Mr. Chairman,

Thank you very much for your May 24th letter replying to my queries on how the decision was reached to build the Brooklyn Heights Promenade. A clipping from the *Brooklyn Heights Press* is enclosed reporting your letter and discussing the unanswered questions that remain.

Inasmuch as the original plans for the Brooklyn-Queens Expressway did not include the Promenade, it remains of considerable historical interest to try to determine by just what process of discussion, argument or compromise the Promenade came to be added to the design. If you should have further recollections of this at any time and would care to pass them on, it would always be a pleasure to hear from you.

Yours sincerely,
Henrik Krogius

Letter from Robert Moses to Henrik Krogius, dated June 13, 1979.

Dear Mr. Krogius,

I realize that the historical background of many of the public improvements made in the City of New York is of great interest, but without digging into the minutes of the City Planning Commission meetings held more than thirty-six years ago, it would be impossible to give you any accurate information on details of the events leading up to the construction of the promenade. I know that I never heard of the Pierrepont proposal until you wrote me. I don't remember Mr. Nitardy, although I was friendly with Mrs. James, and my people were in more or less constant touch with people in the neighborhood.

It would have been impractical and probably illegal to use public funds to build grass plots or front yards for those people fronting the promenade. It certainly was in the public interest, as well as in the interest of the adjacent property owners, to build the promenade as a buffer against the traffic noises emanating from the expressway. It also provided one of the most magnificent views of the harbor and made it available for the general public. Although I have not personally seen it, I have been told that the view has been used by the moving picture and television industries and photographers.

It was a unique design for the highway and was certainly more to the advantage of the community than attempting to blast through it from the vicinity of the Fort Greene Houses to connect with the Gowanus Parkway.

Cordially,
Robert Moses

Letter from S. Starr Walbridge to Henrik Krogius, dated January 30, 1982.

These statements sent to Mr. Krogius by Mr. Walbridge document his memories of the conception, design and construction of the Promenade in Brooklyn Heights.

Cantilevers and Promenade

It was soley [*sic*] my idea to use cantilevers to support Brooklyn Queens Expressway along Columbia Heights, and it was soley my idea to have a cantilevered pedestrian walk, or promenade, above the upper road. These ideas developed as set forth in the following paragraphs.

As Ernest Clark has stated, W. Earle Andrews' office studied six different routes for that section of Brooklyn Queens Expressway between Atlantic Avenue and Washington Street. The shortest was from Hicks Street to Tillary Street, but, along with the others, was abandoned in favor of the Furman Street route. Ernie's records may give you actual dates. I do not now have the dates, nor did I keep a job diary. Nevertheless my recollection of the facts is clear.

So there came a time when our office had determined that the correct route for BQE should parallel Furman Street. After crossing over Atlantic Avenue, the road would swing toward the waterfront. The Fire Department pumping station at Joralemon Street presented a problem. We decided that we could go above its roof and come into the Columbia Heights section well above Furman Street, still having the two roads side by side. This is shown on the enclosed Xerox print taken from a W. Earle Andrews study plan dated February 1943. (Our ultimate design provided for removing, then rebuilding the upper portion of the Fire Department pumping station to accommodate the lower profiles required along Furman Street.)

As field inspections disclosed the character of the area over which we would be building with this arrangement, the two-level section was developed, using columns to support the roads, one directly above the other. Having decided on this arrangement, Earle instructed his draftsman-delineator Julian Michele to prepare sketches to show in perspective how this would look.

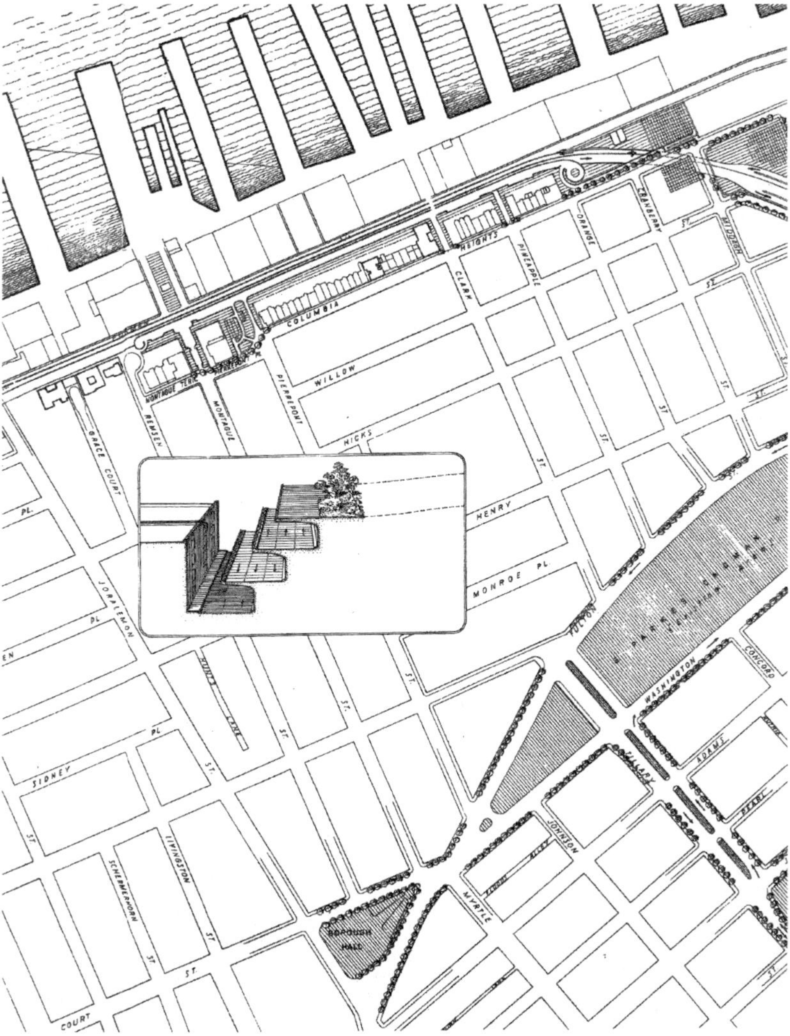

This detail from an Andrews and Clark drawing, dated February 1943—the month before the public hearing at which the design appeared still undecided—clearly shows the triple cantilever in an inset and precisely indicates eventual length of the Promenade, down to its circular ends at Remsen and Orange Streets, as well as the configuration that the main Montague Street entrance was to have. The narrow, fingerlike piers at top were later replaced by wider platforms and pier sheds. Other drawings of the same date show an alternative configuration of the highway essentially on one level, with no promenade deck on top—the version that was the one officially presented at the March 1943 hearing. *Richardson Archive, Brooklyn College.*

Julie came out in the drafting room and conferred with me on this to determine what spacing he should show for the vertical columns which would be required to support the upper road over the lower one. As we discussed this, I told Julie that we could do a lot better than to have all of those columns, and I told him that we should carry the roads on cantilevers, thus eliminating the columns. Julie agreed with me and, at my request, returned to Earle with this recommendation. Earle accepted this transformation, and directed Julie to draw up this proposal.

From this innovation, a next step was to determine the structural and economic limitations for the dimensions of the cantilevers.

Earle felt that a curved form should be used for the undersides of the cantilevers. He said that a curved shape would deflect vehicular noise and fumes away from the buildings on Columbia Heights. This would be all right for the lower road I thought, but the upper road had no such diversion device.

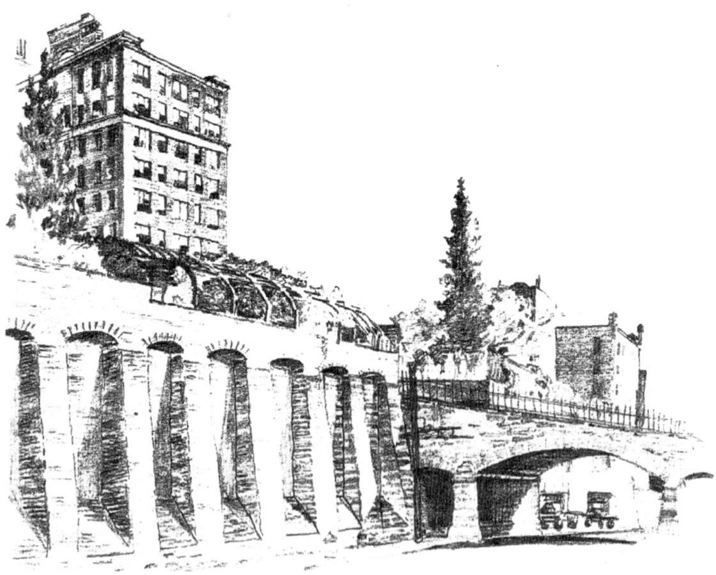

A retaining wall supported the Brooklyn Heights embankment just north of Montague Street, which ran down to the docks with an arched overpass above Furman Street. The apartment building at top is 2 Montague Terrace. This sketch, presumably by Julian Michele, the artist/delineator for Andrews and Clark Engineers, is dated September 17, 1942. *From an Andrews and Clark brochure.*

It was at this point in the development that I proposed an upper deck as a pedestrian walkway, cantilevered over the upper road. This in fact was the birth of the Promenade.

Looking into the profile requirements for this walkway, it was found that we could provide access to it from the ends of the dead end streets.

Parenthetically, since our earliest association in the Spring of 1927, Earle Andrews and I both held firm to the conviction that the best solution to any design problem had not been achieved until it presented the most pleasing final appearance.

So it was with the shape of the underside of the cantilevers. Earle himself developed their shapes, then had those shapes mathematized by his staff.

Then Earle submitted the shapes to the best acoustical engineer he could find to check for the efficacy of those shapes in deflecting noise away from the Heights, and he engaged another expert to provide an opinion on the deflection of vehicular exhaust fumes. I distinctly recall Earle's deep concern that he have a structure that would stand up to the greatest scrutiny. His aim always was to provide Robert Moses with the very best answer to Moses' every request of him.

Michael Rapuano

Michael Rapuano had no part whatsoever in the conceptual design of the triple-cantilevered section of Brooklyn Queens Expressway.

It is possible that Gilmore Clarke conferred with Mike on the landscaping of the Promenade after Earle Andrews asked Gil to take on the task of the design of that landscaping. It was my understanding at the time that the landscaping design was principally the work of Gil's wife.

To my knowledge, the credits which may be claimed for Mike would be only for his having been Chairman of the group entrusted with the assembly and arrangement of the May 1, 1968 report to the Secretary, Department of Transportation, by the Urban Advisors to the Federal Highway Administration. In his Foreword of that volume, Lowell K. Bridwell pointed out that two specific examples documented (East River and BQE) provide a noteworthy step in the right direction to make highways serve society as fully as possible. Brid was Federal Highway Administrator at that time. As you probably know, Brid is Executive Director of the Westway, having been retained for that task by the State of New York. He and I were associated on that project for a while.

One may note that this Report—the Freeway in the City—omits all credits to those who conceived and designed the urban freeways from which Mike and his staff drew their admirable conclusions for "The Systems Approach." This omission makes it easy to infer that the Urban Advisors should be credited with the examples used. Actually, their credits should be limited to the assembly of the material and their participation in the text of the Report.

SHORTRIDGE HARDESTY

W. Earle Andrews, Engineer, was a newcomer on the scene of engineering firms in New York City, and believed that older consulting engineering firms might be critical of his structural design of the new cantilevered structure along Columbia Heights. He knew that the consulting engineering firm of Waddell and Hardesty, and its successor, Hardesty and Hanover, had a superior reputation in the structural design field, especially in bridge design. Shortridge Hardesty himself had an acknowledged reputation as an engineer who was thorough, sound, and conservative, and had many fine bridges to his credit. He was the consultant's consultant. Earle told me that he wanted Shortridge to sign the plans for the detailed structural design of the BQE cantilever structure. At Earle's request Shortridge analyzed the design computation made in Earle's office, and recommended that the cantilever sections be made heavier. Shortridge told me that, while the design was safe and sound, the flexibility at the outer edges of the cantilevers might make some drivers nervous, especially those with heavy loads in those westerly lanes. So he recommended thickening and stiffening the cantilevers. When this had been done, Shortridge signed the plans. This added more concrete and steel bars, modestly increasing the loads and cost, but it was deemed the better way to go.

Ernest Clark, Phillips Lovering and Ernest Pichel did the major design computations for the triple-cantilevered structure. It was this work that Shortridge Hardesty was asked to review and check.

Following this experience with Shortridge Hardesty, Earle Andrews had him associated with him on other projects, both in New York City and elsewhere, both as consultant and as structural designer on bridges.

Incidentally, Shortridge's son Egbert asked me to join Hardesty and Hanover in 1964. I did join as Chief Engineer of Highways and Partner-Designate in February 1965, working with them until my retirement in 1974.

Hastings Block

There came a time when the question arose as to the treatment of the surface of the promenade. Earle Andrews wanted to pave the walkway area with "Hastings Block," an hexagonal asphalt block widely used by New York Park Department before World War II. When Earle tried to find a source of supply for these blocks, he found that their manufacture had ceased. I liked the block, too, and Earle agreed that I should try to get them.

I found Mr. Hastings, for whom the block were named, and he told me that the shortage of asphalt during the war had forced him to shut down his plant, and he had no intention of ever starting up again. In fact, he had retired.

However, I kept after him, and after many conversations and after my assurances that I would require the contractors to buy and use them, and there would be a need for a great many of them, Mr. Hastings acquiesced, agreeing to start his operations as soon as he received the first order. My only reward was that he did indeed make them, much to my satisfaction. They are still being made, I am told.

BQE Under Brooklyn Bridge

There came a time when we needed to know how and where we would run BQE under the approach to Brooklyn Bridge. Earle Andrews sent Julian Michele and me out to make a field inspection to find out what problems would be encountered. It appeared that we could use York Street, but we needed to have more intimate information. Our field inspection gave us the answers, and York Street was used.

During our field inspection, I observed that the then existing buildings along Fulton, Front, and Main Streets hid and obscured the beautiful stone-faced approach to Brooklyn Bridge, and the architecturally charming brick arches under the ramp. I told Julie, and upon our return to the office, I told Earle that the City should acquire the properties so that we could demolish the buildings, dispose of the accumulated trash, and clean up the stone and brick, restoring them for the enjoyment of the public. This was done.

To go through the York Street opening, we had to continue the cantilevered type of construction, modified to fit this opening in the Brooklyn Bridge approach.

Photographer Louise Casey

Tall, erect, perfectly turned out, LOUISE CASEY was a familiar sight in Brooklyn Heights for decades, her jet-black hair eventually turning gray. For the striking photographs she took of the highway and promenade being built in her backyard, I am much indebted. They greatly enrich this book.

I knew her first as the aunt of Emil Froehlich, one of the kids who played along with me on the streets of the Heights in my early years here. It was only much later, after she learned of my interest in the history of the Promenade, that Louise Casey told me of her pictures. She said that she had been given a box camera in her late teens and that she had taken pictures with it while accompanying her parents on trips to Europe and Egypt. She had gone on using it, purely as an amateur and without preserving negatives or really organizing her pictures, and it was with that same camera that she photographed the emerging cantilever structure. Only a few of her pictures were dated.

She lent me her prints to have copy negatives made and to publish prints from them to illustrate my articles about the Promenade's history in the *Brooklyn Heights Press*. To judge from her contact prints, her camera produced relatively large and oblong negatives for a box camera, two and a half by four and one-fourth inches. Even though it was a single-focus camera, without exposure controls, it obviously had a very good lens, leading to surprisingly clear images when enlarged from the copy negatives. And while she was an amateur,

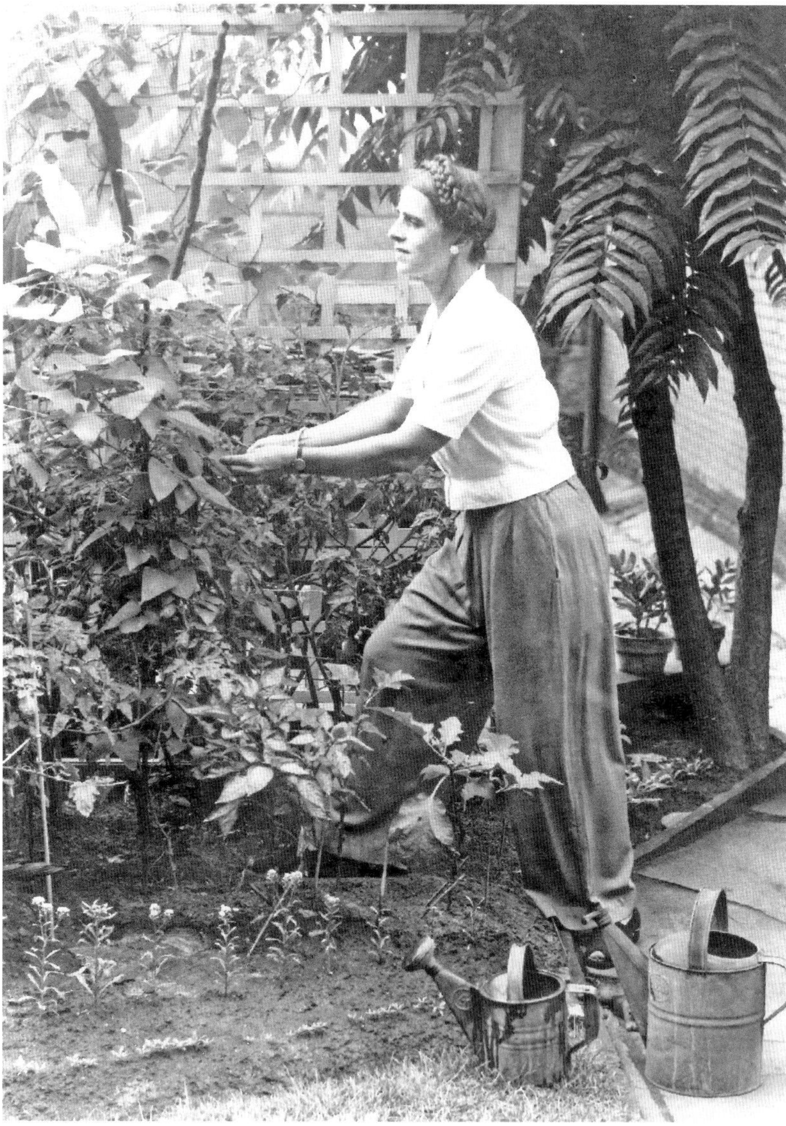

The always elegant Louise Casey, who was to take impressive photographs of the BQE construction more than a decade later, is seen tending her World War II Victory Garden behind 162 Columbia Heights in 1943. She would lose most of her garden to the construction. In 1943, much of her view was, in any event, obscured by warehouses opposite on Furman Street. Brooklyn Eagle *photo.*

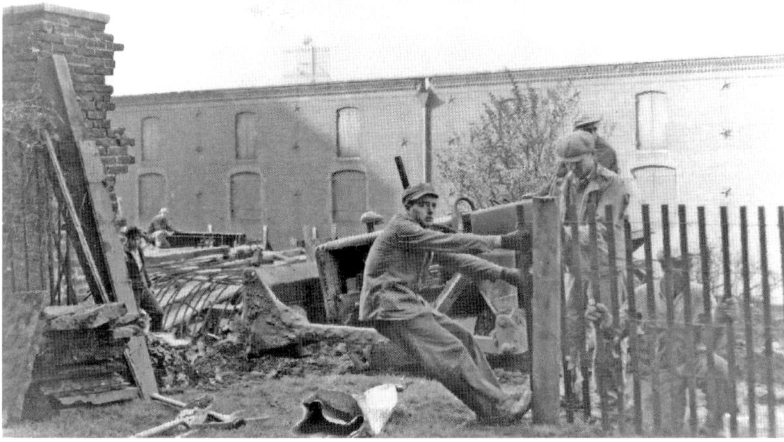

Workers tear down fencing of Louise Casey's garden behind 162 Columbia Heights, as the upper deck of the BQE is seen emerging at left, photo dated November 1948. This was in a day before construction workers wore hard hats. *Photo by Louise Casey.*

Mrs. Casey had a trained eye; she had graduated from Pratt Institute in Brooklyn, a school of art and architecture, and she had been a high school art teacher.

She had moved to her Columbia Heights apartment with her husband, Edward F. Casey, a painter and illustrator, in 1932. Accounts of her precise address there are confused and contradictory, giving it both as number 62 and number 68. However, upon examination of her photographs and the topography of the Heights embankment, as well as the curve of the highway, my conclusion is that she most likely lived at 162 Columbia Heights. By her later years, when she acquainted me with her photographs, she had moved to Remsen Street. She died in June 1988 at the age of ninety.

Among her friends in Brooklyn Heights, Louise Casey was known for her collection of toy birds, especially toy penguins, and a nickname of hers was "Caseybird." The Caseys had no children. A sister, Marie Froehlich of Landrum, South Carolina, and her nephews, Emil and Peter Froehlich, were her nearest survivors. After her death, I had brief contact with Emil, who expressed no interest in the photographs. What has become of her photographs other than those of the highway/promenade construction, I do not know.

About the Author

A native of Finland, Henrik Krogius studied architecture at Harvard and journalism at Columbia. From Columbia, he received a Pulitzer Traveling Scholarship that formed the basis of travel and freelance reportage from Europe, Asia and Africa in 1954–56.

For twenty-seven years, Krogius was employed by NBC as a writer and producer of news. While still with NBC, he began his research into the elusive origins of the Brooklyn Heights Promenade. Building on that research, he received three grants to study the possibilities for a better relationship between urban highways and pedestrians. The grants funded further international travels.

Krogius wrote extensively on these matters for the *Brooklyn Heights Press and Cobble Hill News*, whose publisher, J. Dozier Hasty, invited him at the end of 1990 to be its editor. He has served in that capacity since then. He is the author of two previous books: *New York, You're a Wonderful Town!* (Arcade Publishing 2003), a chronicle of his more than fifty years in the city told through photographs and running text; and Abroad: *Quest and Self-Questioning in a World Gone By* (self-published through Blurb, Inc., 2010), a work about his 1954–56 travels. He is married to Elaine Taylor Krogius, a retired arts librarian. They have two sons and two grandchildren.